Keepin' It Real

My Game Changing Secrets + Shortcuts to Make You Look Like a Queen in the Kitchen

CARLA BUSHEY

inspired girl BOOKS

TABLE OF CONTENTS

Dedicated to all the hot mess mamas, Queen Bees, my amazing family, and people who just want to LOVE life to the fullest!

Hey Queen!

In today's world full of social media and filters, it has finally become the trend to be more real and authentic. I've been waiting for this, because now I feel like I can actually fit in! Don't get me wrong, I love a good filter on a selfie, but real life is not all glitz and glamour. It is running late to get to school (you should see me doing my "walk of shame" a few days a week), helping with homework that you barely understand (what happened to simple math?), being at sports and dance competitions that can take over your life, and often wishing there were more hours in the day to get dishes and laundry done. Anyone else out there grateful for the "wrinkle away" cycle?

If you ask me, I will skip every chore in the house, except for cooking. Why? Not only do I love to cook, but sharing a meal together is my time with my family. That's when I find out how the girls are doing, what bothers them, what makes them happy. I just listen to them talk and I love it more than anything. My mom says I'm the fastest cook because the majority of my meals are done in half an hour, but my goal is to make delicious meals as fast as I can to spend the most time with my family enjoying it together! I am a person who craves simplicity, and the truth is that my dinners don't have to be cooked from scratch so I feel "the approval." After all, wouldn't your kids approve chicken fingers and French fries? Don't be so hard on yourself and try to live up to people's expectations. Stop complicating your life and do what makes your heart happy.

My goal with this book is to help you do that. I'll give you simple and quick recipes that will make your family love you even more. Yes, you WILL be a Queen in the Kitchen! Wear that crown proudly! We are going to take shortcuts and replace ingredients if we are missing them, but I promise you that cooking will be something you will love to do after you try some of my recipes. It is my hope that this book is a total game changer for you when it comes to cooking! Hop on the *Hot Mess Express* and let's whip up something good!

I got your back so don't sweat it, girl 😊

xoxo
Carla

HERE'S THE SCOOP

(like what you'll need and how to use this book!)

TOOLS IN THE KITCHEN: I'm always impressed by all the different gadgets that come out to the market for "specific needs" in the kitchen. Truth is, I'm as simple as it gets when it comes to cooking! Just give me the basics (the needed kitchen tools my grandma and my mom used) and I will whip you up something good! These are my MUST-HAVE tools ☺

- ☐ Measuring Cups & Spoons
- ☐ Cutting Boards
- ☐ Cooking Knives
- ☐ Stand Mixer or Hand Mixer
- ☐ Rolling Pin
- ☐ Wooden Spoons
- ☐ Dutch Oven
- ☐ Loaf Pan
- ☐ Baking Sheets
- ☐ Whisk
- ☐ Can Opener

- ☐ Spatula
- ☐ Pie & Cake Dishes
- ☐ Peeler
- ☐ Grater
- ☐ Mixing Bowls
- ☐ Citrus Squeezer
- ☐ Parchment Paper & Aluminum Foil
- ☐ Colander
- ☐ Silicone Brush
- ☐ Wine Opener (duh!)

CARLA'S TIPS: You know I am sharing all of my game changing secrets + shortcuts with you throughout this entire book! And on some of the recipes I give you even more tips and tricks! These are just some things that I have learned to make cooking even easier and the food even more delicious!

> *"Women's propensity to share is universal.*
> *We confirm our reality by sharing."*
> *~ Barbara Grizzuti*

STAPLES IN THE KITCHEN: There are few things I always keep on hand that literally save my life when I'm having one of those scatter-brained days. These are my go-to ingredients for easy meals that my family loves ☺

Pantry:

- ☐ Pasta
- ☐ Olive Oil
- ☐ Store-Bought Marinara Sauce
- ☐ Chicken & Beef Bouillon
- ☐ Red Vinegar & Balsamic Vinegar

- ☐ Canned Beans
- ☐ Canned Corn
- ☐ Flour
- ☐ Chocolate Chips
- ☐ Oak Hill Farms Honey

Fridge & Freezer:

- ☐ Heavy Cream
- ☐ Cream Cheese
- ☐ Sour Cream
- ☐ Garlic
- ☐ Grated Parmesan Cheese

- ☐ Sausage
- ☐ Ground Beef
- ☐ Chicken Tenderloin
- ☐ Spinach
- ☐ Eggs

To keep your sanity:

- ☐ Wine!

ONE MORE THING! I am from Peru. I wrote this book and intentionally did not edit out my accent! So it might not all be grammatically correct, but just picture me with my Peruvian flair and it will make perfect sense!

Rise 'n Shine

The early bird gets the coffee, isn't that how the saying goes? At least in my world, because catching a worm isn't nearly as tasty. At 5am, I "rise and grind" (and I mean coffee grinds) because I keep telling myself I can't function without caffeine. Not only am I a 6-cups-of-coffee kinda girl, but I can also eat 6 eggs a day like it's nobody's business. From a simple toast with butter and jelly to a hungry man's feast, breakfast is the most important meal of the day. I am guilty of skipping it sometimes, but on the weekends it's go-time! I put my apron on and get all the frying pans going - I don't even care if my hair smells like bacon! Besides, I'm sure my husband appreciates a bacon hair smell (am I right?).

*Raise your coffee cup sisters
and lets get cracking!*

The Best Scrambled Eggs
(According to my Dad)

Scrambled eggs might seem like something so simple to make, but to make them really well and the proper way they should be, is just not as easy as cracking them. I have some simple secrets to do it right, and I will share them!

My dad has always raved about my scrambled eggs. My dad is an attorney, but he's a foodie at heart, and a wannabe chef! He has traveled around and has had food from almost anywhere. He is a tough critic. To hear him say that not even in Paris he has had such amazing scrambled eggs as mine made me smile so big. Every time he comes to visit, he will stay with me and he only has one request, and that's "Carla's scrambled eggs." Even if he comes late at night, or whatever time of day it is, I always make sure I have all my ingredients to make him scrambled eggs as soon as he arrives. (It's never too late at night to make eggs, right?)

My scrambled eggs are made with a lot of care, because I want to make sure that they never get dry on the bottom, and they never get crusty either. So, you have to move them and move them the entire time with a rubber spatula, and you cannot keep your eye away from them. It's like watching a baby, so trust me when I tell you watch those eggs! I also add cheese and heavy cream to make them nice and fluffy. I hope you and everyone in your home enjoy my scrambled eggs as much as my dad does.

MAKES 2 SERVINGS *Prep time* Less than 5 minutes | *Cook time* Less than 5 minutes

WHAT YOU'LL NEED

- 4 large eggs
- 2 tbsp butter
- 4 tbsp heavy cream
- pinch of salt and pepper

LET'S DO THIS!

In a small bowl lightly beat the four eggs while adding the heavy cream, salt, and pepper.

Heat the butter in a small saucepan over medium heat until foamy. The foamier, the better!

Add the egg mixture to the saucepan and continue to move the eggs with a spatula whenever they start to set in the pan.

Cook to desired consistency, remove from heat and serve.

Carla's Tip

I like to use a rubber spatula to stir the eggs. It really helps to avoid them browning on the bottom. The rubber tip spatula really makes a HUGE difference!!

Fun 'n Fab French Toast Roll Ups

This is a dish I started making when my kids were very little, on Christmas morning, so they would have something different and fun to eat. I never thought that I would be making this Christmas after Christmas for 18 years now (am I aging myself?), and they still love it just like when they were tiny. The filling makes it so good, and sooo different. It's smooth, sweet, and creamy and goes nice with the cinnamon sugar crust that gets a little caramelized when you cook it. No worries, if you don't like cream cheese (I don't know how that's possible but I hear it's a thing), you can always substitute with other fillings, like fruit jams or Nutella, but my kids just like the sweet cream cheese that I have always put in it! Now they make it with me, and it is a Christmas morning staple. They look forward to opening presents and to have Fun 'n Fab French Toast Roll Ups afterwards.

MAKES 10 SERVINGS   *Prep time* 5 minutes | *Cook time* 15-20 minutes

WHAT YOU'LL NEED

- 1 loaf white bread, the thin slices
- 1 block cream cheese, softened
- ¾ cup powdered sugar
- ¾ cup granulated sugar
- 1 tbsp cinnamon
- ½ cup melted butter

LET'S DO THIS!

Cut off the crust of the bread, and with a rolling pin flatten the bread.

In a small bowl, combine the cream cheese and powdered sugar. Mix until well blended.

In a separate bowl, combine the granulated sugar and the cinnamon. Set aside.

Spread 1-1 ½ tbsp of cream cheese mixture onto each flattened bread piece and roll it up, Queen!

Dip each piece of rolled bread into the melted butter and then into the cinnamon sugar mix. Ooh, my mouth is watering already!

Place all the bread pieces on an ungreased cookie sheet.

Bake at 350°F for 15-20 minutes or until golden brown. Serve warm with Oak Hill Farms Maple Syrup. SOOO good!!

Grandma's Scones

This is probably one of my most favorite recipes in the book. It has definitely given me a run for my money. It was no easy feat!! It took me like a whole year of Sundays to perfect this recipe, but it was worth every flour-filled second. I have made these scones Sunday after Sunday nonstop until I was able to get the perfect mix of ingredients. It is an original of my grandma's but of course she didn't have it written down as a recipe, so I was going based on memory of the taste, and I have tweaked it to make it savory or sweet. Hers were sweet only. I don't want to sound bossy, but when I tell you to never over-mix, over-knead, or under-chill just listen to me—okay, I guess I sounded a little bossy. All jokes aside, if you follow these 3 important tips your scones will be the talk of the day, maybe even the week! I make it for every brunch I host and every big holiday I have. If you fail the first time do not give up, because when you do get it right you will feel so proud and accomplished, just like I did. I'm telling you it is like letting the soul of your inner Julia Child out in the kitchen!

MAKES 8 LARGE SERVINGS OR 16 SMALL SERVINGS

Prep Time 30 minutes | *Cook Time* 25 minutes

WHAT YOU'LL NEED FOR THE SCONE BASE

- 2 cups all-purpose flour
  (plus more for kneading)

- ⅓ cup granulated sugar

- 1 tbsp baking powder

- ½ tsp salt

- 6 tbsp unsalted cold butter
  (cubed into tiny pieces)

- ½ cup heavy cream
  (plus more for brushing)

- 1 large egg

- 1 tsp pure vanilla extract

Mix It Up and Have Some Fun with these Variations!

BLUEBERRY LEMON: Add 1 cup of fresh blueberries and 1 tbsp of lemon zest

LEMON GLAZE: 1 cup powdered sugar and 1 tbsp lemon juice.

CRANBERRY ORANGE: Add 1 cup of fresh cranberries and 3 tbsp of orange zest.

ORANGE GLAZE: Add 1 cup powdered sugar and 3 tbsp orange zest.

CHERRY CHOCOLATE CHIP: Add ¾ cup of chopped fresh or frozen cherries and ¾ cup of chocolate chips.

VANILLA GLAZE: Add 1 cup of powdered sugar, 2 tbsp milk, ½ tsp pure vanilla extract.

LEMON POPPY: Add the zest of 2 lemons, and ½ tbsp of poppy seeds.

CINNAMON SUGAR: Add tsp of cinnamon to taste plus coarse sugar after brushing with heavy cream.

HAM AND CHEDDAR: Reduce sugar to 2 tbsp, leave out pure vanilla extract, add 1 cup of cooked cubed ham, and 1 cup of shredded cheddar cheese. Sprinkle sea salt after brushing.

LET'S GET THAT SCONE BASE GOING!

Preheat oven to 400°F.

Line a large baking sheet with parchment paper and set aside.

In a large bowl, whisk together the dry ingredients: flour, sugar, baking powder, and salt.

Add the tiny CUBED COLD BUTTER (this is very important!) and using a pastry cutter or two forks cut into the dry ingredients until you have small pea size crumbs.

In a separate mixing bowl, whisk together the wet ingredients: heavy cream, egg, and pure vanilla extract until well combined.

Add wet ingredients to the dry ingredients. *If you are making any of the variations add the ingredients now* and stir JUST until combined. It should be crumbly at this point.

Put this mixture onto a lightly floured surface and knead it just enough to form it into a ball.

To make triangle scones, flatten the dough ball into roughly an 8-inch circle. Cut the dough into 8 equal wedges. If you want to make the smaller scones, do the same process but make two 4-inch dough balls instead of an 8-inch piece.

Put it into the freezer covered in plastic wrap for 5 -10 minutes. *DO NOT SKIP THIS STEP!*

Take the dough out of the freezer and brush it with heavy cream.

Bake it off at 400 for 18 – 25 minutes, or until golden brown around the edges and lightly browned on top.

Carla's Tips *Girlfriend, it all comes down to this!*

1. Do not substitute the heavy cream - if you do, you will end up with a flat scone.

2. Make sure your butter is really cold, I mean really, really cold. This is what makes an explosion in the oven and makes the scones right.

3. Do not over-knead your dough, this will make a harder scone, and please be patient when you have to chill. Grab a glass of wine, sip it, enjoy it, and just relax. Let your dough chill while you chill. No chugging 😊

My Hubby's Breakfast Bowl

This breakfast bowl was born out of a lack of breakfast meats and a hungry husband. Let me explain. When Rich and I just got married, I would get up and make him breakfast religiously every weekend. He is a meat and potatoes kind of guy. So, I would always make sure that I had plenty of sausage, bacon, or pork roll 😊. When I woke up and went to make him breakfast, I realized that not only was I shy on meats, but I didn't have any tater tots or leftover potatoes to fry up. Luckily, I was able to scrounge a few potatoes and onions from the veggie basket and some peppers from the fridge. I chopped them all up, seasoned them really well (a little bit on the spicy side) and baked them off. I threw the only two sausage links I had in the frying pan. When those potatoes came out of the oven, I sliced up the sausage and mixed them all together with an unhealthy portion of cheese. I served this in a bowl and topped it off with two fried eggs. From that moment on weekend after weekend I would hear, "Hey honey, will you make me my breakfast bowl?" Guess the lack of breakfast meats didn't matter so much after all!

MAKES 6 SERVINGS   *Prep time* 15 minutes | *Cook time* 25 minutes

WHAT YOU'LL NEED

- 1 recipe of the "Little Cubes of Happiness" potatoes

- 6 large eggs, fried

- 8 breakfast sausage links (can substitute with bacon if desired)

- 1 cup shredded cheddar cheese

Follow the instructions for the "Little Cubes of Happiness" to see how to make the potatoes

LET'S DO THIS!

In a skillet add the sausages with a few tbsp of water on high heat. Don't worry, the sausages will have enough fat to evaporate the water and should brown evenly.

Five minutes before the potatoes are ready to come out of the oven, slice the sausage or bacon and add it to the potato mixture, along with half a cup of the shredded cheddar cheese. Mix it all up and place back in the oven for the remaining five minutes.

When the potatoes are finished in the oven, place in a bowl, add more cheddar cheese (because you can never have too much cheese, right?!) and top it off with a fried egg and serve! Happy Hubby, and you look like a Queen!

Busy Bee's Honey Granola

They say that breakfast is the most important meal of the day, but let's face it, we all have such busy lives we don't always have time for a big meal in the morning. Oh, how I love a nice breakfast! In Peru, breakfast was very different. I had fresh squeezed juice, anything I wanted made fresh with fresh ingredients, it was an experience. And I didn't have to cook it back then, I just got to enjoy the goodness. Okay, but I moved to America when I was 18, and for a while I went the opposite direction and would grab a bowl of Cocoa Puffs and call it a day. I could only imagine my family's reaction to sugar-coated cereal in a box!

I eventually came back to my homemade roots, though. But who has time for a total fresh squeezed breakfast every day in the states? Plus, reality hit when my kids started growing up and they were in a rush to get out the door for school. So, I decided to make breakfast an easier task on everyone. I wanted to keep them healthy and well-fed so I started making my own honey granola—not nearly as fancy as it sounds! I will wake up early on Saturday or Sunday (while everyone at home sleeps and I get my peace and quiet), and I will start baking my honey granola. It takes me only half an hour to make, but it also takes off so much of my morning mom stress.

This recipe is super simple, filling, and nutritious. We love our honey granola over plain Greek yogurt, with steel-cut oatmeal, or even sometimes we just add a handful to a little plastic baggie and have something to munch on throughout the day. I make a week's worth, and I keep it in a big glass jar on my kitchen shelf. It is so delicious that sometimes instead of lasting for a full week, it only lasts for two or three days. Don't tell me I didn't warn you!

WHAT YOU'LL NEED

- 3 cups old-fashioned oats (rolled oats)
- ½ cup sliced almonds
- ½ cup pecans, halved
- 1 tsp ground cinnamon
- ¼ tsp nutmeg
- ½ cup coconut oil, melted
- ¾ cup Oak Hill Farms Honey
- ¾ cup dry cherries, raisins, or cranberries (you can also mix them all)
- Optional: ¼ cup chocolate chips

LET'S DO THIS!

Preheat the oven to 350°F.

Line a big baking tray with parchment paper. In a large bowl mix together the oats, nuts, cinnamon and nutmeg.

In a small bowl, mix together the coconut, oil, and the honey. I like to pop my coconut oil into the microwave for 15 seconds so I can get it melted, that way it will mix well with the honey! Is your mouth watering yet?

Pour the honey mixture over the oat mixture. Mix and stir evenly until everything is coated nice and good.

Pour the honey oat mixture into the baking sheet, using a spatula to spread evenly over the tray.

Bake for about 25-30 minutes, stirring halfway through. Remove the tray from the oven and the granola will harden while it cools. And it smells so good!

If you want clusters of granola, once you've take it out of the oven do not stir the granola until it is completely cool. This way it is easier to break it into chunks.

If you're not sure that the granola is ready you can do the clink test. Use a spoon to remove a few pieces of granola and set them into a glass. Wait a few minutes for the granola to cool then shake the cup. If the granola clinks, then it is done. If the granola doesn't clink leave it to bake for a few more minutes before you test again.

Once the granola has cooled, transfer it to a big bowl. Break it apart and mix in the dry cherries and chocolate chips if desired. This mixture can last for a few weeks if it is kept in an airtight container and it is so good on the go!

Little Cubes of Happiness

I took a trip with my husband to Fells Point Maryland, where we celebrated his 49th birthday (I should highlight that I am 10 years younger than him 😊). Since it was his last year in his 40's, I wanted to choose a place that he would truly enjoy, and Fells Point is a quaint town on the water, known for having the best seafood. He loves seafood AND being on the water, so this was going to be a perfect destination. After having a few Bloody Mary's and mimosas (Hey, we're partying! It's vacation!) we got our main course for brunch, and both of our dishes came with these tasty, well-seasoned home fries.

After Rich saw his dish, he told me that his grandma used to make the same kind of home fries and she called them "little cubes of happiness". It's funny, I've made those so many times before at work and growing up, but I guess I never made them for him! Realizing it brought back happy memories for my husband, I decided to make them more at home. I'm happy to share my recipe so you guys can enjoy these Little Cubes of Happiness, too!

WHAT YOU'LL NEED

- 4 tbsp olive oil

- 4 tbsp salted butter

- 1 cup yellow onions,
  diced into small pieces

- 1 cup red peppers seeded,
  cut into small pieces

- 8 medium to large red potatoes,
  skin on and cubed

- 2 tsp coarse salt

- 2 tsp black pepper

- 1 tsp smoked paprika

LET'S DO THIS!

Heat the olive oil in a skillet over medium/high heat. Don't let it smoke!

Add the onions and peppers, then cook until brown about 5 minutes. Do not let these burn, stir frequently. When done, remove from the heat and transfer to a bowl.

While the onions and the peppers are cooking, add the potatoes into a large sauté pan. Add just enough cool water until the tops of the potatoes are covered and they start floating slightly.

Place the pan over high heat. As soon as the water begins to boil, remove it from the heat and drain the potatoes into a colander (this takes about 5 minutes).

Place the pan where the onions and the peppers were sauteing back onto the burner on medium to high heat and add the butter. When the butter starts to foam, add the potatoes on a single layer, making sure they all touch the surface of the sauté pan. Listen, happiness takes time, love, patience, and attention! But it will be soooo worth it!

Allow to cook for about 3-4 minutes without stirring so they all get nice and brown. Then flip them and do the same on the other side.

Once all the sides are nice and crispy add the onions and peppers back to the pan, stir gently and add salt, pepper, paprika. Remove from heat and serve!

Jersey PEC Breakfast Sandwich

One of New Jersey's staples is a good breakfast sandwich with pork roll—not something we have in Peru! If you live up in north Jersey you might know it as Taylor Ham, but down by the beach we call it pork roll. And by the way, we are correct because Taylor Ham is a brand name of pork roll! It's like instead of saying, "Can you pass me the toothpaste?" Hello. We are right.

The love my kids have for pork roll is insane. At any bagel shop, pork roll, egg, and cheese is the breakfast sandwich of choice. If they go to a diner, a Jersey burger will be their choice just so they can have a slice of pork roll on top. They are even willing to line up for 2 hours at a school food truck festival just to get a pork roll, egg, and cheese sandwich.

Let me go deeper into that story, I remember like it was yesterday. When my Sophia was a freshman in high school, they had this big food truck fest at her school with all kinds of international foods. The options were endless, but of course, my child had to line up for her beloved pork roll, egg, and cheese sandwich. We stood for two hours in a not-moving line!!! (I don't know what the heck they were doing to this pork roll in that food truck.) But you had to see my baby's happy face shining through in the middle of the school's parking lot. It was priceless! So now, I make a variation of this breakfast sandwich with my famous scrambled eggs, on Hawaiian bread, and of course with extra pork roll slices! ☺

MAKES 12 LITTLE SANDWICHES

Prep time Less than 5 minutes | *Cook time* 15-20 minutes

WHAT YOU'LL NEED

- 8 slices pork roll

- 12 count package of Hawaiian rolls

- 6 slices American cheese

- 6 eggs

- 4 tbsp butter, divided

- salt and pepper to taste

- 3 tbsp heavy cream

LET'S DO THIS!

Preheat the oven to 350°F.

Prep a 9x13 baking sheet with aluminum foil. Slice the Hawaiian rolls in half lengthwise and place the bottoms on the sheet (do not pull the rolls apart).

In a sauté pan over medium heat place the pork roll slices, searing on both sides. This takes about a minute per side.

Cut the pork roll slices in half and place an even layer over the bottom of the buns.

Make scrambled eggs in a skillet over medium heat. To do that, whisk the eggs, heavy cream, salt and pepper and cook in one tablespoon of butter. Make sure to leave them runny because they will finish cooking in the oven.

Add the eggs on top of the pork roll, cover with a layer of American cheese, place the bun tops on, melt the remaining butter and brush on the top of the buns

Heat in the oven for 15 minutes, serve and enjoy!

Zucchini Bread with Chocolate Chips

2015 was the year that I decided to start my own garden at home. Rich and I moved the year before to start a life closer to nature, and I had the chance to google every kind of gardening tip and idea I could find. The inner Barefoot Contessa in me had big plans to have the best garden anyone can dream.

I planted a lot of vegetables and a few fruits, and I failed on a lot of them! (It's easy to look back and laugh about it now. Yes, I am blushing 😊). But there was one thing that I grew very well that year, and that was zucchini. I actually overgrew zucchini. I had zucchini everywhere in my garden. I even had zucchini growing under my garden, and going around my chicken coop. So, as you can imagine my chickens had a big feast that summer! I had to search for every zucchini recipe and put it to use. My dinner menu consisted of zucchini noodles, zucchini lasagna, zucchini boats, zucchini gratin, but the only thing my kids seemed to like was my zucchini bread. Once I added chocolate chips, it was a game changer! And it's very simple!

Prep time 10 minutes | *Cook time* 55 minutes

WHAT YOU'LL NEED

- 1 ½ cups all-purpose flour (spoon and level)
- ½ tsp baking powder
- ½ tsp baking soda
- ½ tsp salt
- 2 tsp ground cinnamon
- ¼ tsp ground nutmeg
- ½ cup vegetable oil
- ½ cup packed brown sugar (light or dark will work)
- ½ cup granulated sugar
- 1 large egg at room temperature
- 2 tsp pure vanilla extract
- 1 cup shredded zucchini
- 1 cup semi-sweet chocolate chips

LET'S DO THIS!

Preheat the oven to 350°F. Then grease a 9x5 inch loaf pan or use a non-stick 9x5 loaf pan.

In a large bowl, whisk the flour, baking powder, baking soda, salt, cinnamon, nutmeg, and chocolate chips together until truly combined. Set aside.

In a medium bowl whisk the oil, granulated sugar, brown sugar, egg, vanilla, and zucchini together until well combined.

Pour the wet ingredients into the dry ingredients and gently whisk until JUST combined, do not over mix. This batter will be semi-thick.

Spread the batter into the loaf pan and bake for 45 to 55 minutes. I would highly recommend to loosely cover the loaf pan with aluminum foil halfway through the cooking process to avoid heavy browning on top.

The bread is done when a toothpick inserted in the center comes out mostly clean without having any batter on it!

Remove the bread from the oven and set aside. Allow to completely cool before slicing.

Carla's Tip

If you have anything left after you slice, you can actually store it at room temperature for 3 to 4 days, or in the refrigerator for up to one week! But of course, it doesn't last more than 10 minutes in my house!

Mama's Brunchin' Pie

This is a traditional French recipe but it came to my hands from my Peruvian mother. Every Tuesday she would get together with a group of lovely ladies for brunch. They would take turns hosting these brunches to plan fundraisers, charity events, and functions at church. These ladies happened to be the moms of all my friends in the neighborhood. I have the most amazing childhood memories with this group of friends, and hold them all so dear to my heart.

When it was my mom's turn to host brunch, she would start preparing the night before. She would make the prettiest hors d'oeuvre's, cut the fruit to perfection, set up an impeccable table where she would show off her best China and silverware, and finish it with some fresh blooms from her garden. Every detail counted. I think my love for home décor, entertaining, and paying attention to the details definitely comes from her.

One of my favorite recipes she made was her bacon and cheese quiche, or as she would call it with her cute French accent, "Quiche Lorraine" (Fun fact: My mom studied French and was a French teacher.) When I go for brunch and I see Quiche Lorraine on the menu that is my go-to. Not only because I love the dish, but it brings me back to the memories of seeing my mom whipping up her best recipes in the kitchen I grew up in.

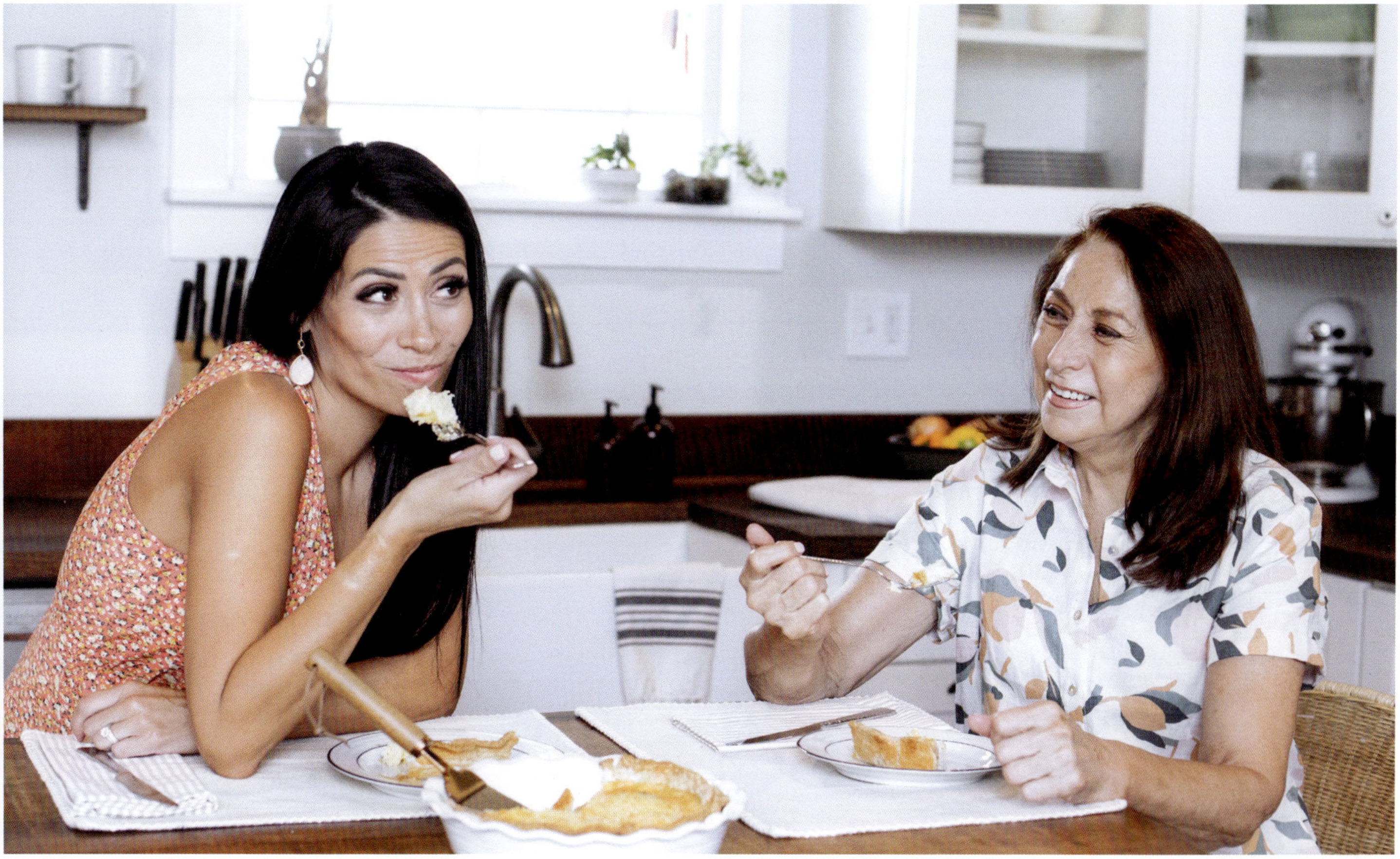

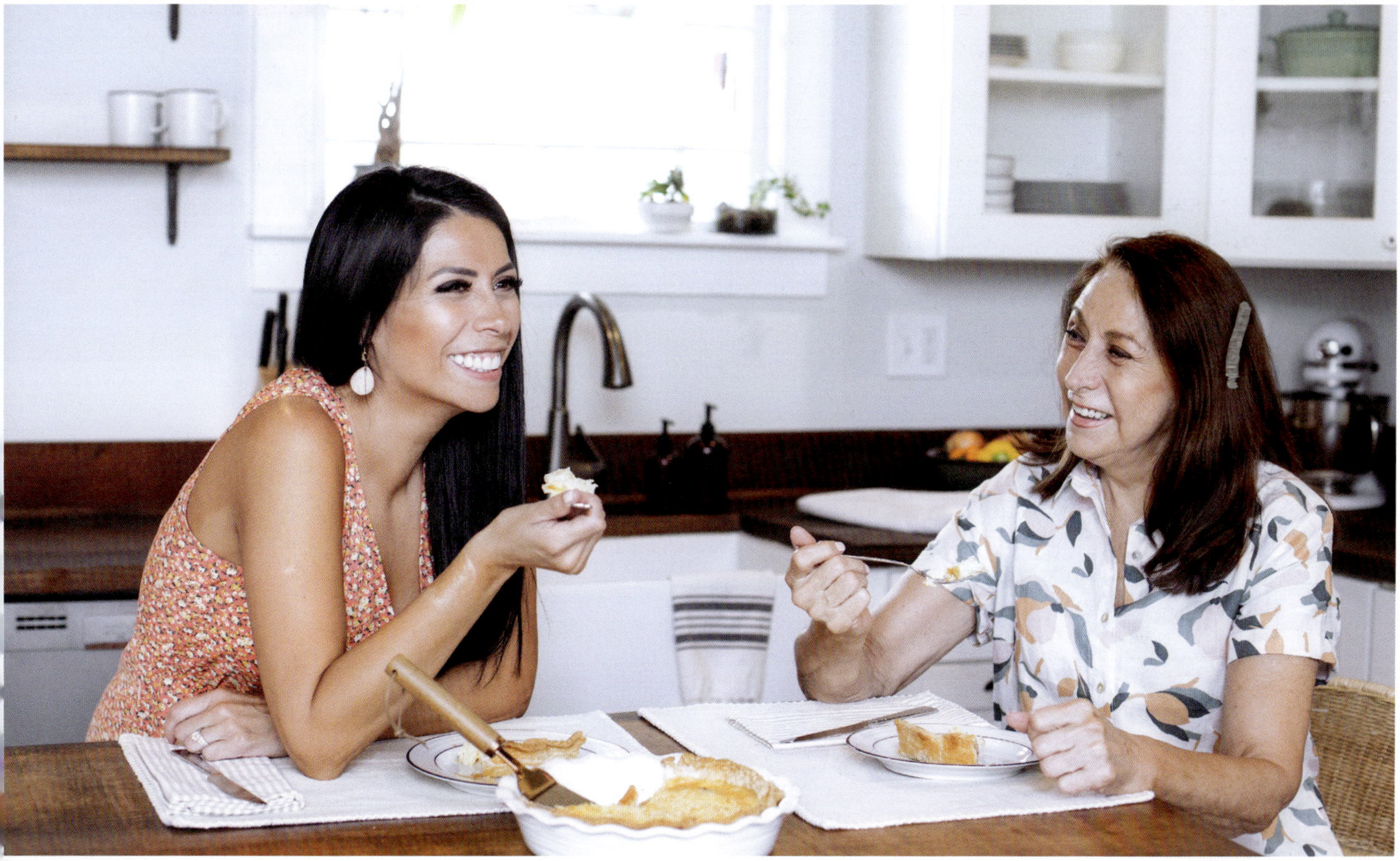

MAKES 6 TO 8 SERVINGS *Prep time* 5 minutes | *Cook time* 45 minute

WHAT YOU'LL NEED

- 1 pie crust (for a 9-inch pie)
- 4 pieces bacon, diced
- 1 onion thinly sliced
- 1 cup Gruyère cheese or Swiss cheese, shredded
- ¼ cup grated Parmesan cheese
- 4 eggs lightly beaten
- 2 cups heavy cream
- ¼ tsp nutmeg
- ½ tsp salt
- ¼ tsp fresh ground black pepper

LET'S DO THIS!

Preheat the oven to 400°F.

Line an 9-inch pie dish with the pie crust. Make sure you build a rim with the pie crust - this will create a wall for when you put the custard inside.

Cover the bottom of the pastry with a round piece of parchment paper, add some dry beans for weight to avoid the pie crust raising while it bakes off. Bake off for 10 minutes.

Once you take the pie crust out, reduce the oven heat to 375, discard all the beans and the parchment paper, and set the partly cooked pie crust aside.

In a skillet, cook the bacon (in its own fat) until crisp. Pour off the fat grease from the skillet but leave about 1 tablespoon worth. Cook the onions in the remaining fat until they become transparent.

On the pie crust, sprinkle the cooked bacon, onions, and the cheese all over evenly.

In a separate bowl, combine the eggs, cream, nutmeg, salt, and pepper. Mix really well. Strain this mixture over the pie crust, filling the pie crust with it.

Put the filled pie crust on top of a baking sheet and bake for about 25-30 minutes. Then check the quiche by inserting a knife about 2 inches from the rim of the pie crust. If the knife comes out clean it is ready to serve! And you will probably eat the whole thing!

Liked it — would use less heavy cream and more eggs next time!

My Take on Avocado Toast

Do you know how every time you watch a show like Shark Tank, you feel like you have one of those ideas that people bring to the show, and you say after they sign them, "Dang it, if I showed that same idea or an idea similar to that, I would be a millionaire right now!" That's exactly what happened with avocado toast. I could have been the trendiest person if I decided to share that recipe a few years back before it was everywhere. Of course, avocado toast is one of the most popular takes on toast today, something that they have on every fancy brunch menu. But it was really just a version of something so simple and cheap that I grew up on: "Pan con Palta."

I have memories of growing up—my brother and I being dragged to my grandmother's house every Saturday for "lonche." In Peru, lonche is a small meal around 6pm that consist of coffee, tea, and a sandwich or pastry.

My grandma would send the kids to the corner market to get the ripe avocados, and then we would run to get warm fresh bread from the bakery right out of the oven. We would make coffee, tea, milk, and juices for the kiddos. We would put out a big bowl of smashed avocados, with simple ingredients like salt, pepper, and lime in the center of the table, and everyone would serve that avocado on their own toast.

In today's world, avocado toast will get dressed up with salad on top, fancy seasoning or oils, honey or glazes, but mine still remains very simple, with just some of my favorite ingredients on a good piece of bread and a fried egg on top!

MAKES 2 SERVINGS   *Prep time* 5 minutes

WHAT YOU'LL NEED

- 1 large avocado
- ½ lime, juiced
- 2 thick slices whole wheat bread
- salt and pepper
- Optional: a fried egg to put on top. Salt and pepper can be replaced with an "Everything Bagel" seasoning that is also very tasty

LET'S DO THIS!

Toast the slices of whole wheat bread. Sometimes if I have a rustic bread, I cut slices and I put them into the toaster or I bake them off.

While the bread is toasting, slice the avocado in half and remove the pit. Scoop out the flesh into a bowl and mash it very well with a fork.

Add the salt and black pepper to taste.

When the toast is ready, spread the mashed avocado generously onto each piece.

Serve while the toast is still hot!

Iced Caramel Latte

I really don't have much to say about this recipe, besides the fact that I make my own Iced Caramel Latte only to avoid my children from spending their entire week of earnings at a fancy coffee shop! 😊 Actually, if it was up to me I would never drink an iced coffee. I like my coffee only hot, maybe it's a cultural thing. Growing up in Peru I couldn't imagine drinking coffee cold AND spending a small fortune to do it! However, I will treat myself to a whipped coffee as a dessert.

MAKES ONE SERVING   *Prep time* *Less than 10 minutes*

WHAT YOU'LL NEED

- 4 oz strong brewed coffee, cold brew or shot of espresso (chilled)

- ½ cup half and half

- 2 tbsp caramel
  (I use Oak Hill Farms Original Goat's Milk Caramel for this recipe)

- ice cubes

- Optional: whipped cream and more caramel to drizzle

LET'S DO THIS!

Brew your strong coffee, or make your espresso shot and chill it, or you can use cold brew.

In a glass, mix the half and half with the caramel and mix it well.

Using a handheld frother, froth it until it becomes foamy.

Pour this mixture into a glass with ice and add the chilled coffee on top!

You can garnish with whipped cream, and drizzle caramel on top.

My Kinda Chai

I owe my love for chai tea to one of my best childhood friends: Fiorella. We grew up in Peru together, and both moved over to the states! Years back Fiorella lived in Florida, and she wanted to further advance her career in finance. She felt it was necessary to move to a bigger city with more opportunities in her field, so she ended up moving to New Jersey. Oh, how exciting to have my best friend here. Now I'm sure you know how the rest of this story is going to go ... Fiorella moved in with me and it was one of the best times in my life. My children were only toddlers and having Fiorella with us (or Fifi as my kids would call her) was like having an auntie at home. We were inseparable and did everything together. She even became my mom's best TV buddy and would watch Law and Order marathons every night with her (my mom seriously needed a new buddy because I can't watch any more than five minutes of a show without falling asleep).

Now, getting back to the chai because I could honestly write a book about Fiorella—she was the one who got me hooked. Every time you'd see her, she was holding a cup of chai. Every coffee shop she went into, she would order chai. If we went out for breakfast, she would order guess what ... chai! Even at home she would make her own chai. Since then, I have tried making different chai recipes. I have shared many of those on Instagram, and on my blog, but definitely this one is the winner. It is a simple mix of the perfect amount of spices that makes it convenient, tasty, and inexpensive. Raise your chai and become a fan just like I did.

MAKES ONE LATTE   *Prep time* Less than 10 minutes

WHAT YOU'LL NEED

Chai Spice mix

- 1 tbsp ground nutmeg

- 1 tbsp ground ginger

- 1 tbsp ground clove

- 2 tbsp ground cardamom

- 2 tbsp ground cinnamon

To make the latte

- 3 oz half and half

- 1 tbsp chai mix

- 2 tsp honey

- 1 tsp pure vanilla extract

- 8 oz black steeped tea

LET'S DO THIS!

In the microwave or a little saucepan warm up the half and half with the honey and the pure vanilla extract. Using a handheld frother or an actual frother pitcher, froth this mixture until nice and foamy, add the hot black steeped tea and enjoy!

Honey Latte

I never thought that honey and coffee would go well together. Actually, I never thought of honey as a big deal until my husband decided to become a beekeeper. Yes, I said a beekeeper, and yes we live in New Jersey, and yes he is not from a farm town, but boy was it a fun learning curve. Lots of boo boo balm (this is our own homemade version of a first aid ointment and maybe I'm inspired to write a book about these kinds of recipes now, but you'll have to wait on that one!). We were collecting so much honey that I decided to replace all the sugars I was using with honey. I was baking with honey, I was sweetening all my drinks with honey, and I even started to learn how to cook with honey. You will get to see more of those recipes in this book, just be a little patient, okay? Just kidding! My love for honey grew almost as much as my love for coffee so I thought, what better way to enjoy them both than to pair them together. That is when I came up with my Honey Latte recipe, which is by far my favorite and everyone else's at home. Honey takes the bitter of the coffee and makes it sweet, but not too an extreme—it's the perfect amount of sweetness, and froths great with milk. I don't know maybe it is just me, but I think it is simply delicious and I hope you enjoy this recipe as much as we do. Plus, it's easy peasy.

MAKES ONE SERVING

Prep time Less than 5 minutes | *Cook time* Less than 5 minutes

WHAT YOU'LL NEED

- 6 oz milk of choice
- 4 oz strong brewed coffee or one shot of espresso
- 1 tbsp pure honey (Oak Hill Farms is the best!)
- 1 tsp pure vanilla extract

LET'S DO THIS!

Mix the pure vanilla extract and the honey into the milk.

Warm on the stove or in the microwave if in a hurry. Who isn't in a hurry sometimes, right?!

Once the milk is warm, use an automatic or handheld frother and get the milk nice and foamy.

Once the milk is frothy, pour it into your desired cup. Pick your favorite cup!!

Add 4 oz of strong brewed coffee or espresso shot and serve.

Whipped Coffee

If you grew up in a Latin American country, it probably wasn't even discussed whether it was appropriate or not to give coffee to your children. I grew up on coffee and have been drinking it as long as I can remember. It is part of my culture and every single morning I would start my day drinking café con leche. And yes, my kids drink coffee now too. It's funny because this recipe, which was very popular last year and all over social media, was pretty much what I grew up on. Even though I only used a spoon to make this concoction and now people use a mixer (so fancy!), it was pretty much the same idea. You can have it either hot or cold, as a morning wake me up, or drizzle some honey on top like I do and have it as a treat. I hope you like this recipe and if you allow your children to drink coffee, I won't be responsible if they are up all night. 😊

MAKES ONE SERVING

Prep time Less than 5 minutes

WHAT YOU'LL NEED

- 2 tbsp instant coffee

- 2 tbsp granulated sugar

- 2 tbsp warm/hot water

- 6 to 8 oz milk choice
  (hot or cold)

- Optional – Oak Hill Farms
  Honey to drizzle on top

LET'S DO THIS!

In a bowl mix together the instant coffee, water, and sugar. Using a handheld mixer or whisk, whisk until it becomes the consistency of whipped cream.

In a glass, pour your milk of preference over ice, simply cold or even hot (whichever you prefer because it's all about YOU and what you love!).

Then pour the mousse-like coffee on top, very delicately so it doesn't fall on the bottom.

For extra sweetness, you can drizzle a little bit of honey!

Dips 'n Things

One of the things I enjoy the most is having parties. I mean, I was always a party girl growing up...and I always look for any excuse to have a celebration. Come on, am I the only mom who throws elaborate graduation parties for their children coming out of pre-k? 😆 I think I get that from my grandma. She was the happiest person in the world always looking to make a big deal of even the smallest achievements her children and grandchildren had. We would always get together, have a nice meal, and to start the party: tons of appetizers! I love carrying on her title of *Party Queen!* Celebrating life is what it's all about, right? I host parties all the time and I like to show off a little with different varieties of appetizers to keep my guests happy and full. There's just something about a good appetizer that can set the mood for the entire party. I love seeing my guests dive-in and stuff themselves. Seriously, by the time dinner comes, they all wish they wore sweatpants with a stretchy waist! They don't call me an entertaining PRO for no reason!

Here are some of my fan-favorite go-to dips and things that I love to make...

Jalapeño Popper Dip

You may know by now, I love to entertain. I love to have people over, I like to make long lasting memories, I love to cook, I love to dance…why not, right? Having parties at home and hosting parties is something that comes very natural to me. I always try to change up my appetizers because the same group of friends come around and I wanna make sure to stay trendy. I don't want to give them the same ole same ole, ya know? I don't have to go crazy, I just switch it up a tiny bit so people always get a little surprise and never know what to expect at the next Carla party.

My daughter Sophia loves spicy food! On one occasion we were hosting a party (I can't remember specifically why we were having this party, but there is always a reason to party!). I was going to make my traditional appetizers that day, but Soph asked me to change things up. She wanted me to make something a little more on the spicy side. So, she inspired me to make this Jalapeño Popper Dip. It is super simple and very creamy and cheesy. You can serve it with toast, chips, or crackers. It goes well with all. It was something that people didn't expect to have but it was a pleasant surprise. When I created it I just called it Jalapeño Popper Dip because it had all of the elements of that fun appetizer. So, we can thank Soph for suggesting to put a little spice in our life because now this is one of our favorites, and we hope it is one of yours as well!

MAKES 6-12 SERVINGS   *Prep time* 10 minutes | *Cook time* 15 minutes

WHAT YOU'LL NEED

- ½ lb bacon, cooked and crumbled
- 16 oz cream cheese, softened
- ½ cup sour cream
- ½ cup mayonnaise
- 1 cup shredded cheddar cheese
- 1 cup shredded mozzarella cheese
- ¼ cup sliced green onions
- salt, pepper, garlic powder to taste
- 7 jalapeños, seeded and chopped or ½ cup canned jalapeños, chopped

LET'S DO THIS!

Preheat the oven to 350°F.

In a large mixing bowl add the cream cheese, sour cream, mayo, and garlic powder. Stir until smooth.

Fold in the crumbled bacon (reserve 1 tablespoon for garnishing), add in half of the shredded cheddar, half of the shredded mozzarella, jalapeños, and green onions (reserve one tablespoon for garnishing).

Transfer the mixture to an oven safe baking dish, about eight to ten inches round or square, sprinkle the remaining cheddar, mozzarella, bacon, and onions on top. Bake for 15 to 20 minutes until heated through—melted and bubbly—and serve.

Hot Hoagie Dip

Tommy and Silvana Edwards have been our best friends for a very long time. Tommy and my husband Rich have been working together for over 15 years and they have built a beautiful friendship that makes them more like brothers. I always joke around with my husband and tell him that Tommy is his second wife, and that he calls him more than he calls me throughout the day. The Edwards have a really beautiful and inviting home, and they love to host the group of couples inside our friend group. All the wives will make either appetizers or desserts and Silvana, because she is hosting, will always take care of the main meal.

On one occasion our friend Sharon brought this delicious hoagie dip. Now if you're not from South Jersey or Pennsylvania, you may not know what a hoagie is, but boy are you missing it. Picture the best hot sub stuffed with meat and cheese. Alright, now imagine that as a DIP! Genius.

I don't know where she got the recipe from but she always has creative and clever ideas in the kitchen. I never heard of a hoagie dip and I was hesitant to try it. Then I had my first bite. It was on top of a little piece of toast perfectly buttered. The mixture of all the Italian meats with cheese coming fresh out of the oven, it was just out of this world. I couldn't stop telling Sharon how delicious it was and I knew I wanted that recipe. From the top of her head she gave me the ingredients. Later when I recreated it at home I tweaked it to make it my own version. I love when recipes come out of gathering with amazing friends and can be shared with the people you love.

WHAT YOU'LL NEED

- ¼ lb ham, diced

- ¼ lb pepperoni, diced

- ¼ lb salami, diced

- ¼ lb capicola, diced

- ½ lb provolone cheese, diced

- 1 cup shredded mozzarella cheese

- 2 blocks cream cheese, softened

- ½ cup mayonnaise

- seasoning: 2 tsp dried oregano, 1 tsp garlic powder, salt and pepper to taste

- toppings: 2 or 3 Roma tomatoes, diced, ½ cup chopped pepperoncini's, ½ a head iceberg lettuce, finely sliced

- To serve – one large baguette, crostinis, pita chips or crackers

LET'S DO THIS!

Preheat the oven to 350°F.

In a small bowl, combine the softened cream cheese with the mayonnaise, and add all the seasoning.

Add all the diced meats, diced provolone, and half of the mozzarella to this cream cheese mixture and mix until everything is well combined.

Pour everything into a 9x13 oven-proof baking dish, top with the other half of the shredded mozzarella cheese, and bake at 350°F for twenty to twenty-five minutes.

Once the dip comes out of the oven, add the chopped tomatoes, sliced pepperoncini's, and right before serving, add the sliced iceberg lettuce.

Serve with crackers or bread of choice.

Rancher's Buffalo Chicken Dip

You may be thinking "Buffalo Chicken Dip? Been there, done that, have the recipe already!" I get it! I have probably seen over 100 variations of this recipe on Pinterest but I think mine is really good and different. Maybe because we are "ranchers" here, I made a minor substitution with the traditional bleu cheese, but it makes a major change in the flavor!

I mean I don't want to sound braggy, but my kids say that mine is by far the best one they've ever had. Alright, well maybe they are a little bias because I am their mother and they just really love my cooking, but I want to believe it is the truth. This is my daughter Gianna's favorite dip by far! She has been the Buffalo Chicken Dip Queen at home for the last two years. Every time we decide to entertain, or the girls have to bring something to somebody's house she always wants to make Buffalo Chicken Dip. I'm actually starting to think that more than anything it is because she takes spoonful's before she starts baking it off. Honestly though she knows the recipe by memory. She is always the one making it and it has become her staple now. I hope you find this variation as good as we think it is, and it can become a staple for you as well.

MAKES 6-8 SERVINGS *Prep time* Less than 10 minutes | *Cook time* 20 minutes

WHAT YOU'LL NEED

- 32 oz canned chicken pre-cooked chicken (can also substitute with shredded rotisserie chicken or shredded poached chicken)

- 16 oz cream cheese

- 1 cup ranch dressing

- ¾ cup buffalo sauce (I like Frank's hot sauce, or Frank's buffalo sauce)

- 2 cups shredded cheddar cheese

LET'S DO THIS!

Preheat oven to 400°F, soften the cream cheese by leaving it out 30 minutes before you begin (if you are in a rush girl, just remove the wrapper and microwave in a safe bowl for 1 minute).

In a mixing bowl, add the chicken, cream cheese, buffalo sauce, ranch dressing, and 1 cup of the shredded cheese (reserve the other cup to top it off).

Combine the mixture until it is nice and smooth, then add the mixture to an oven safe dish. Sprinkle the remaining cheddar cheese over the mixture and bake for 20 minutes or until the cheese starts to brown.

Serve nice and warm with chips, toast, cut vegetables, or whatever you prefer.

G's Loaded Deviled Eggs

I love eggs. I mean, I really love eggs. I can have them any way - scrambled, fried, made into an egg salad, as a quiche, in an omelet, oh my mouth is watering just writing about it!! But on the daily, hard-boiled are my go-to. They are so easy. However, for holidays, deviled eggs are the star of the show. I make my deviled eggs very simple, but my kids have taken those simple recipes to another level. They have lots of variations on the deviled egg, and one of our favorites was concocted by my daughter Gianna. She came up with the loaded deviled egg.

When I asked her what makes it loaded, she replied, "Have you ever heard of a loaded baked potato? Same idea, Mom, just instead of a potato it's an egg!" She said it with her little "sass", like, "Duh, Mom! Don't you get it?" But really, she is so smart! When I tried her recipe with the creamy filling of the deviled egg and the added chives and bacon it was a total game changer! It makes me so happy to see her whipping up my recipes with her own little upgrade and making them better than Mom does. And she let me add the recipe to this book, so YAY for you, too!

MAKES 24 DEVILED EGGS   *Prep time* *10 minutes*

WHAT YOU'LL NEED

- 12 large eggs, boiled, cut in half (remove yolks and save for preparation)
- ½ cup mayonnaise
- 6 strips bacon cooked crisp and crumbled
- 2 tbsp chopped chives, divided
- ½ cup shredded cheddar cheese, divided
- salt and pepper to taste
- 1 tsp yellow mustard
- 2 tsp Worcestershire sauce

LET'S DO THIS!

Slice the eggs in half lengthwise, removing the yolks and placing in a medium sized bowl. Place the egg whites flat on a serving platter.

In the bowl with the egg yolks, add the mayo, two-thirds of the crisp bacon, half of the chopped chives, half of the cheddar cheese, salt, pepper, yellow mustard, and Worcestershire sauce.

Mix until well combined.

Fill each egg white with the yolk mixture.

After filling, top with the remaining bacon, chives, and cheddar cheese.

Sweet 'n Sassy Montecristo Sliders

A ham and cheese sandwich is always underappreciated, but luckily I have my Aunt Tata to remind me just how tasty they can be. She visits me often and she will make them pressed as paninis, open faced on the stove, or simply just cold. I think it's about time to give the ham and cheese sandwich the credit it deserves!

Ham and cheese is usually a savory sandwich, but this recipe packs a sweet surprise!! If you don't know which way to go, savory or sweet, the answer is: make Montecristo Sliders and your problem is solved. Mixing these flavors is the best of both worlds. The saltiness of the ham and Swiss cheese with the sweetness of the powdered sugar and the raspberry sauce for dipping makes this sandwich perfect for any party! If you're entertaining, you can make it ahead of time. Bonus!! And it's a perfect addition to any brunch or tea party.

MAKES 12 SLIDERS   *Prep time* Less than 10 minutes | *Cook time* 25 minutes

WHAT YOU'LL NEED

- 12 count package Hawaiian rolls

- 12 thin slices ham
  (I like to use black forest ham)

- 12 thin slices turkey

- 12 slices Swiss cheese

- 2 tbsp Dijon mustard

- 1 large egg

- ¼ cup melted butter

- powdered sugar for topping

- raspberry or strawberry
  jam/preserves for dipping

LET'S DO THIS!

Preheat the oven to 350°F. Spray a baking sheet with non-stick cooking spray.

Slice the Hawaiian rolls in half lengthwise, but do not pull the rolls apart. Spread the Dijon mustard on each slab of rolls.

Layer the sliders as follows: half of the sliced cheese on the bottom, sliced ham, sliced turkey, the remaining cheese on top. Add the bun tops.

In a small bowl combine the melted butter with the egg. Whisk it together and brush the top of the rolls. Cover the rolls on the baking sheet loosely with aluminum foil, without letting the foil touch the bun tops to avoid sticking. You can use toothpicks if necessary to make sure the foil doesn't touch the top of the buns.

Bake at 350°F for 15 minutes. Remove the foil and bake for another 10 minutes until the tops are nice and golden brown. Sprinkle with powdered sugar and serve with your choice of jam or preserve for dipping.

My Secret Guacamole

Guacamole is not just a dip to me, it's an appetizer!! And it's one of those appetizers where I will always make a double or triple batch. I will actually cross my fingers hoping that nobody eats it or that it's not the appetizer of choice on the table so I can have it all for myself (I get pretty greedy when it comes to guacamole). The main ingredients to make it are very simple. However, what makes it a secret guacamole is this valuable piece of information I'm about to give you: the secret to keeping it green! Some people think it's the citrus of the lime, some people say to cover with plastic wrap and not serve it until all of your guests arrive. I'm telling you right now, I can have my guacamole out for three hours and it never turns brown.

Are you ready to know the secret?

It's so simple but so overlooked! Don't ever, ever throw out the pit. Grab a glass of drinking water–no specific size or color, no magic glass, just a glass. Put all the pits of the avocados that you are using in there and fill it with water. It sounds crazy and I know you will tell me that it is an old wives' tale, but just try it and you are going to believe me. I have no clue how the secret got into my family's hands, but I just remember my mom telling me and me laughing at her. After realizing it worked, I passed the secret on to many people. People would laugh at me and then call me after and they would say, "Car, you are so right!" I don't know why, but it works!! And I'm not going to even pretend to get all science-y on you. Just try it! If you want a delicious guacamole follow my recipe, and if you want to keep it green just put the pits in the water.

MAKES 6-8 SERVINGS   *Prep time* 5 minutes

WHAT YOU'LL NEED

- 3 ripe avocados peeled and pitted
- 1 jalapeño cored, finely diced (add more or less depending on taste)
- ½ cup red onions, finely diced
- 1 Roma tomato cored, and finely diced
- 1 tbsp fresh lime juice
- ¼ cup fresh cilantro, finely chopped
- ½ tsp salt
- ¼ tsp black pepper

LET'S DO THIS!

In a medium mixing bowl, using a fork mash the avocados until your desired consistency (I like mine a little chunky).

Stir in the jalapeño, onion, lime juice, cilantro, salt and black pepper until well mixed.

Add the tomatoes.

Taste the salt and add more if desired.

Serve with chips and enjoy!

Sheet Pan Nachos

I made these Sheet Pan Nachos for the first time years ago for a Super Bowl Sunday. Let's be real. I do all of the cooking so I just wanted something easy peasy for this one, and what is easier than throwing everything in one pan? It was just like that, and turned out to be a true crowd pleaser. Now I love to make them on a busy weeknight because I can serve the entire dish in the middle of the table and let everyone do their thing. This mama deserves a break sometimes and not worrying about who wants extra jalapeño or who doesn't like tomato just takes the load off of me. They can all pick and choose what they want and how much. When I make it, you don't hear a word at the table, only the crunch of the nachos being eaten. My favorite version is with pulled pork but you can make it with chicken, beef, or simply keep it vegetarian by not adding any meat. Regardless of how you have it, you are not going to regret making it because it so delicious!

MAKES 8 SERVINGS   *Prep time* 10 minutes | *Cook time* 10 minutes

WHAT YOU'LL NEED

- 2 cups Spiced Soda Pulled Pork (I usually make these nachos with the leftover pulled pork that I share in this book, but you can make them with ground beef, chopped chicken or any other preferred meat)

- 12 oz tortilla chips

- 1 15 oz can black beans, drained and rinsed

- 1 cup shredded cheddar cheese

- 1 cup shredded Jack cheese

- 2 Roma tomatoes, diced

- 2 jalapeños, thinly sliced

- 2 tbsp fresh chopped cilantro

- ¼ cup sour cream

- Optional: ¼ cup sliced black olives

- Other garnishes: salsa and guacamole

LET'S DO THIS!

Preheat the oven to 400°F.

Lightly oil a baking sheet, or coat with a non-stick spray, or you can also cover with aluminum foil.

Place the tortilla chips in a single layer onto the prepared baking sheet. Top with the pulled pork, black beans, and cheeses spreading them evenly. Place in the oven and bake until heated through and the cheeses have melted, about ten minutes.

Top with the diced tomatoes, sliced jalapeños. Drizzle with sour cream and the chopped cilantro.

If you would like black olives, you can also add them at this point. I serve with a bowl of guacamole and salsa.

OMG I'm Obsessed Bruschetta

A few years back, my brother and I decided to treat my mom because she is just the best and totally deserved it! So, we took her to Italy for her birthday. My brother was living in Germany at the time, and we decided to meet halfway in Rome. We just wanted to give her a long weekend of memories that would last a lifetime. My expectations of Italy were high, and I heard a lot of people raving about different things, like the wine, gelato, or pasta. All were really good, but I'm telling you what I have to rave about is the quality tomatoes they have and how obsessed I became trying their famous tomato bruschetta. It is nothing like the bruschetta you get from a jar in Jersey!

Restaurant after restaurant I was dreaming about this tomato bruschetta. It is something so simple, but I guess it's the fact that they use real ingredients. The tomatoes are perfectly ripe, the bread is grilled or baked immaculate, the olive oil, the simple seasoning, and the fresh basil— oh wow, just a mixture of delicious goodness. If we sat down for lunch, I would have tomato bruschetta, for dinner it would be my appetizer every place I went. When I tell you that I tried maybe ten different tomato bruschetta versions at different places I am actually cutting myself a little short. Italy definitely didn't disappoint. When I came back home, I just wanted to figure out how to do it the same way. I was on a tomato bruschetta kick for a month! I perfected this simple bruschetta that I absolutely adore, and I also adore my mother and my brother and all those amazing memories we made in Italy that weekend.

MAKES 6-8 SERVINGS *Prep time* 15 minutes | *Cook time* 5 minutes

WHAT YOU'LL NEED

- 8 Roma tomatoes
- ¼ cup fresh basil
- ½ tsp dry basil
- 4 garlic cloves, minced
- ¼ cup olive oil (plus more for brushing bread)
- 3 tbsp balsamic
- ¼ tsp salt
- ¼ tsp ground black pepper
- 1 French baguette
- grated Parmesan cheese

LET'S DO THIS!

Preheat the oven to 375°F.

Finely dice the Roma tomatoes, and julienne the fresh basil removing the stems.

In a bowl combine the tomatoes with the fresh basil, garlic, olive oil, dry basil, balsamic vinegar, salt, and pepper. While you cut the bread, allow this mixture to sit in the fridge for 10 minutes.

Cut the bread into ½ inch slices and arrange on a baking sheet. Brush the bread with olive oil and add the grated parmesan cheese. Put it in the oven for 5 minutes, or until the cheese is a little melted.

Remove from the oven and scoop the tomato bruschetta mixture over the cheese crostinis.

Get Your Greens In

Have you ever heard someone say, "I am craving a salad so badly!" and then wondered how can anyone crave a salad? Well, believe me, I have! I grew up on boring salads. I mean . . . really boring! Lettuce, tomato, and onion was "the thing." If I got lucky, my mom would toss a few cucumbers in. ☺ Growing up in Peru, a country where meat and double starch is the norm, salads were always downplayed, or maybe my mom just downplayed them (sorry, Mom, I sold you out). I wanted to change the boring greens and make them fun for my girls. So with a little creativity, veggies of every color, and a good vinaigrette to dress it up, I came up with many salads that my family love. Now my girls get their greens in, and my mom titled me "Salad Queen." Yes, in our family there is a Queen for everything! And I wear those crowns proudly! Oh! And guess what? My girls are now those girls that I never understood, who actually crave a salad.

So, grab your best pair of tongs and have some fun with fruits and veggies!

Fresh 'n Fruity Spinach Salad

For me it has always been a struggle trying to feed my children more vegetables. Mama's out there, please tell me I'm not alone? They are fruit lovers, but vegetables are something that they have never been very fond of. As they were getting older, I started making a lot more salads and adding fruit. It was my attempt to make a simple salad a little more appealing with more than just vegetables. And I was right to do that, because they love this Fresh 'n Fruity Spinach Salad so much!

MAKES 6 SERVINGS   *Prep time* 15 minutes

WHAT YOU'LL NEED

Salad

- 10 oz baby spinach

- 3 apples, cored and thinly sliced
  (I like to use gala or honey crisp)

- 1 cup toasted pecans, or candied pecans

- ½ cup feta cheese crumbled
  (I prefer to buy it in a block and crumble it
  myself. It really does taste so much better!)

- ½ cup dried cranberries

- ¼ cup red onions, sliced thinly into strips

- Optional: 12 oz bacon, cooked and
  crumbled

Maple Cider Vinaigrette

- ½ cup olive oil

- ¼ cup apple cider vinegar

- 2 tbsp Oak Hill Farms Maple Syrup

- 2 tsp Dijon mustard

- salt and pepper to taste

LET'S DO THIS!

Add all the ingredients into a mason jar, cover with the lid and shake really well until everything is mixed, or it can be mixed with a whisk in a bowl.

Slice the red onion and place it in a colander and run it under cold water for about fifteen seconds, dousing it really well. This removes the harsh bite of the onion! Drain well and dry.

In a large salad bowl, toss together the spinach, apples, pecans, cranberries, and the onions. This is where you will also add the crumbled bacon if you choose to! Yum!

Drizzle the desired amount of dressing on top coating evenly. Serve immediately after adding the dressing.

Carla's Tip

Swap out the fruits to match the seasons and you'll enjoy this fresh 'n fruity salad all year long!

Beyond Your Basic Balsamic Vinaigrette

I really don't have much to say about balsamic vinaigrette besides the fact that making it homemade is a game changer! I don't really love to use store bought dressings; I know they come in handy but making your own will take your salad to a completely different level. And it's easy peasy even though the ingredients are so surprising! You can make a big batch of this tasty vinaigrette and keep it in your fridge. Enjoy!

MAKES 2 CUPS   *Prep time* Less than *10 minutes*

WHAT YOU'LL NEED

- ½ cup aged balsamic vinegar

- ½ cup extra virgin olive oil

- 3 tbsp Oak Hill Farms Honey

- 2 tsp Dijon mustard

- 2 garlic cloves

- ¼ cup sun-dried tomatoes

- salt and pepper

LET'S DO THIS!

Pour all the ingredients into a blender, mixing well until completely smooth like velvet-y smooth!

Keep this dressing in a mason jar in the refrigerator and use as needed.

If you prefer your vinaigrette more on the sweet side, you can add an extra tablespoon of honey.

This dressing will keep in the refrigerator for two to three weeks! It's so good on just about everything!!

Carla's Tip

You can use this balsamic recipe as a base and have so much fun with it! Blend in blueberries for a blueberry balsamic, rev up the sweetness with raspberries, make it peachy keen with fresh peaches!

Giga's Chicken Salad on a Pita

My mom is the master of a good chicken salad, and I think that the quality of ingredients used is the key! I have lived more than half my life in the United States. When I first came here, I was very confused, and I felt it was very weird that people would use so much mayo AND from a container? I grew up on homemade mayo. I had never gotten any mayo that came in a container. I know it sounds crazy but that's how it was. Mayonnaise is actually really easy to make and that's one of the first things my mom taught me how to do. We do consume a lot of mayo back home in Peru, but I guess it's just one of those condiments that is just so natural there.

When I was a senior in high school, the school moms decided to have a fundraiser. They set up food stands on our school property, and they would take turns doing kind of like a bake sale. They would sell different foods and all the proceeds would go to our class. The money would be used for us to have extra trips or class parties. My mom was in charge of making a sandwich for the sale, and I remember she chose to make something a little different. It was the traditional chicken salad, but she would alter it by adding raisins, or sometimes she would put grapes cut in half, maybe chopped walnuts, or chopped pecans. She would even slice spinach very thinly to add. She would mix everything up with a homemade mayo of course and stuff it on pita bread. It was very different, very tasty, and is something that has stayed with me forever. This is my mom's super tasty recipe for chicken salad on a pita!

MAKES 6 SERVINGS   *Prep time* 10 minutes

WHAT YOU'LL NEED

Salad

- 2 lbs boneless/skinless chicken tenderloin (cooked and shredded)
- ½ cup diced walnuts
- 1 cup mayonnaise
- 1 cup red grapes quartered

- 2 stalks celery finely diced
- ½ cup golden raisins
- 1 cup fresh julienne spinach
- salt and pepper to taste
- 6 pita breads

Mayonnaise

- 2 large eggs
- 1 tsp lemon juice
- 1 tsp white vinegar

- ½ tsp salt
- ½ tsp mustard
- 2 cups oil

LET'S DO THIS!

Make the Chicken Salad

In a large bowl add all of the ingredients, add the mayonnaise and mix until everything is well combined.

Let it chill in the fridge until you are ready to serve! Easy peasy!

Make the Mayo!

In a blender, add the eggs, lemon juice, vinegar, salt and mustard. Start blending, and with the blender running, slowly drizzle the oil until the mixture is emulsified and thick. (Adding the oil slowly makes for a creamier mayonnaise. The total pouring time to aim for should be 60-90 seconds.)

Carla's Tips!

1. If you are in a hurry you don't have to make your own mayo, store bought will do.

2. If you do make your own mayo, make sure you cover it with plastic wrap while storing in the fridge.

3. Another great option for this chicken salad is to add diced apples.

4. You can also serve this chicken salad on toast, over a bed of greens, as a wrap or lettuce wrap.

Our Staple Honey Vinaigrette

We've been beekeepers for almost a decade and as you can see, I use honey in a lot of my recipes. This honey vinaigrette is the winner in my house for sure and I make it several times a week. This dressing goes really great with any salad. It is so simple that my girls will whip their own vinaigrette in the morning to take with them to school for their lunch. My only recommendation is that you shake it up real good right before you serve it, so the oil doesn't separate. The key is that you use a high-quality honey, like Oak Hill Farms Honey.

MAKES 1 PINT   *Prep time* 5 minutes

WHAT YOU'LL NEED

- ½ cup Oak Hill Farms Honey

- ⅓ cup apple cider vinegar

- ¾ cup extra virgin olive
  (if you don't like the strong flavor olive oil you can always substitute for vegetable oil)

- 2 tbsp lemon juice

- 1 tsp salt

- ¼ tsp black pepper

- Optional for extra flavor: 1 tsp paprika, 1 tsp ground mustard, and 1 tsp ground onion

LET'S DO THIS!

You can either blend all these ingredients together in a blender or simply add them to a mason jar, close it tightly and shake really well. Either way it's perfect!

You can store it in a mason jar in the fridge for up to two weeks. Just be sure to shake it very well before using so the ingredients don't separate.

Nanny Lucy's Lentil Salad

I am a lover of all things legumes, maybe because I grew up on lentils? You see in Peru, we are very superstitious, and people say that if you eat lentils on Mondays, money will never be tight. Guess what I ate every Monday? Lentils! There has to be something to this superstition because my dad provided a beautiful life for us. My Nanny Lucy would have to get creative and make lentils in many different ways. She would make them in stew, soup, or even salads— very similar to the one I'm about to share. The citrus vinaigrette makes it so refreshing mixed with the vegetables, and it is a great way to change things up for a summer barbecue. I'm so glad my nanny is one of the ones who loves to think outside of the box, because we can thank her for this delicious recipe!

MAKES 6 SERVINGS *Prep time* 10 minutes | *Cook time* 20 minutes

WHAT YOU'LL NEED

Salad

- 1 cup dry brown lentils
- 2 Roma tomatoes, diced
- 1 small red onion, diced
- 1 cucumber, seeded and diced
- ½ bunch parsley, finely chopped
- Optional: 2 oz feta cheese

Vinaigrette

- 1 lemon, juice and zest
- ¼ cup olive oil
- 2 garlic cloves, minced
- salt and pepper to taste
- 2 tbsp red vinegar

LET'S DO THIS!

Cook the lentils according to the package direction. They vary a little, but for the most part you are going to bring 3 cups of water to boil in a pot and add the lentils, continuing to boil for about 20 minutes until the lentils are tender. You don't want them to be over cooked because you want them nice and firm for your salad.

Drain the cooked lentils in a colander and rinse them briefly under cool water.

While the lentils cook prepare your vinaigrette. Zest the lemon and cut it in half. Use all the juice!

Mix it with the rest of the ingredients, olive oil, red vinegar, minced garlic, salt, and pepper.

Prepare your vegetables: tomatoes, onions, and cucumbers diced up real nice. Then mix the vegetables with cooled lentils and the vinaigrette.

Add the lemon zest. If you choose, add the crumbled feta and serve immediately!!

Aunt Zoila's Mouth Watering Mango Salad

A few years ago, I went to Peru with my mom and the girls. On this trip we were able to visit my Aunt Zoila and my Uncle Juancho. They are not my aunt and uncle by blood, but it feels like it because they were my next-door neighbors in the house that I grew up.

My Aunt Zoila and my mom built this tight friendship that still stands to this day. Their daughter Romina is one of my best friends, and their son Juan Diego was very close to my brother as well. My Aunt Zoila always goes out of her way to impress us with what she's preparing. That summer night she made different meats on the grill, all kinds of appetizers and desserts, but what really caught my attention was her mango salad. Believe it or not something so simple like a salad that carries the right ingredients can allow you to show off. If I am remembering correctly, I think I had three or four helpings, and I blushed every time I went for more. I can remember that night like it was yesterday, I think there is something so special about making memories with family and friends around the table. She may not have known it at the time, but that simple salad recipe has left a lasting impression on me, and now has made its way into this book to be shared with you and your families.

MAKES 6 SERVINGS   *Prep time* 10 minutes

WHAT YOU'LL NEED

- 8 slices thick cut bacon, crumbled

- 1 small red onion thinly sliced

- 12 oz baby spinach

- 2 mangos, peeled and diced

- ½ cup queso fresco, crumbled

- salt and pepper to taste

- honey vinaigrette

LET'S DO THIS!

In a large bowl mix the spinach with the mango, cheese, and onions.

Add the bacon and toss it well and add a little bit of salt and pepper.

Add the honey vinaigrette right before serving and mix it well and enjoy!

Carla's Tip!

For this specific recipe, I like to pop my honey vinaigrette into the microwave for about fifteen to twenty seconds so it's nice and warm and it adds a great contrast between the fruit and bacon. Salty and sweet, hot and cold . . . ooh, you're going to love it!

Give the Wife a Break Flatbread

Have I told you yet that my husband doesn't cook? Like hardly ever? Actually, it's pretty funny because his friends say that I have spoiled him rotten and he just got comfortable. When I met him, he was so self-sufficient: his home was spotless, he did his own laundry, and he cooked for himself. Guess he fooled me! He even cooked for me once or twice as a little date night. I do have to say though that this flatbread is his creation, so I won't take credit for it. We just like to come home on a Friday night, after a full work week and enjoy a nice glass of pinot grigio by the pool and he will make these flatbreads on the grill. Ladies, don't even read the recipe, go show it to your husband and tell him to fire up the grill. We deserve a break!! Should we put them on laundry duty too?

MAKES 1 FLATBREAD *Prep time* Less than 10 minutes | *Cook time* 5-10 minutes

WHAT YOU'LL NEED

- 1 piece naan bread
- 3 tbsp goat cheese
- 4 thin slices prosciutto
- ½ pear, cored and very thinly sliced
- honey or hot honey to drizzle
- ½ cup baby arugula
- salt and pepper to taste
- 1 tbsp olive oil

LET'S DO THIS!

Place the flatbread on the grill at 350°F. Leave it just long enough to get grill marks on both sides–should take about 30 seconds on each side.

Spread the goat cheese on top of the warm flatbread, then place the prosciutto slices, and then add the thinly sliced pears.

Place the flatbread back on the grill and cover the grill allowing the flatbread to retain the heat

Cook for about 1 to 2 minutes. Check to make sure the flatbread is not getting too dark on the bottom, then remove from the heat.

In the meantime, in a separate bowl mix the arugula with salt, pepper, and the olive oil. Mix it all up and when the flatbread comes off of the grill, add the mini arugula salad on top.

Drizzle with honey on top (or if you'd like a little kick, try some hot honey!).

Rulebreaker Pasta Salad

The first few years right after culinary school I worked in an Italian restaurant. I started working in the salad and dessert station, moving my way up to being the executive chef in the kitchen. When I started, we had a signature tricolor pasta salad that had Caesar dressing as the base. You know unruly Carla, once I became executive chef, I had to make that salad my own. This is so different from all the other pasta salads that people usually serve. The pesto makes it stand out, but it blends well with any summer barbecue. This is my signature pasta salad. It is always a favorite among my family and friends. Can't wait for you to try it!

MAKES 8 SERVINGS *Prep time* 10 minutes | *Cook time* 10 minutes

WHAT YOU'LL NEED

- 1 box tricolor rotini, or tricolor penne pasta
- 2 Roma tomatoes, diced
- ½ cup sliced black olives
- 1 cup baby fresh mozzarella, cut in quarts or halves
- ¼ cup fresh basil, julienne
- 1 tsp garlic, minced
- ½ cup pesto
- 1 cup mayonnaise
- salt and pepper to taste

LET'S DO THIS!

Boil the pasta per box instructions, just make sure the pasta is el dente!

In the meantime, dice your tomatoes, baby mozzarella cheese, and julienne the basil.

In a separate bowl, mix the mayonnaise, pesto, garlic, salt, and pepper until well combined.

When the pasta is cooked and cooled, add the mayo mixture along with the rest of the ingredients and mix really well!

Cover and keep in the refrigerator until it is time to serve.

The Beekeeper's Berry 'n Watermelon Salad

This watermelon salad puts a fun twist on a regular fruit salad. During a nice hot summer day, watermelon is our fruit of choice, but I tend to get tired of only serving it by the slices. This is a fun version where I chop up some watermelon pieces and add all kinds of berries: sliced strawberries, blackberries, and blueberries. I marinate them with some honey and a little bit of balsamic vinegar, and wow, what a difference that makes! I make sure I put it in the fridge before I serve it so it's nice and cool and it really does the trick on a summer day. It's just so sweet and refreshing, and no need to peel all of that cantaloupe!!!

MAKES 6 SERVINGS   *Prep time* 10 minutes

WHAT YOU'LL NEED

- 5 cups watermelon, cubed
- 2 cups strawberries, sliced
- 1 cup blueberries
- 1 cup raspberries
- 1 cup blackberries
- juice 1 lime
- 2 tbsp Oak Hill Farms Honey
- 1 tbsp balsamic vinegar (if you find balsamic glaze at the store that works even better)
- 2 tbsp thinly sliced fresh mint

LET'S DO THIS!

In a large bowl, combine all the fruit.

In a separate bowl, combine the lime juice, honey, balsamic vinegar (or glazed). This combination tastes so good! Pour this mixture over the fruit, then sprinkle the fresh mint on top.

Let it cool in the fridge until it is ready to serve.

Carla's Tip!

If you have leftovers, don't let them go to waste! Mix it all up in a blender and make a smoothie, or add a little of your favorite spirit and make it a cocktail!

Oh-So-Amazing Ambrosia

I honestly don't know if we should call ambrosia a salad or a dessert? My girls love it because of the marshmallows! I totally get it, because if you gave me the choice of having a salad with marshmallows when I was growing up, I would say, "ambrosia every single day!" Mine is very simple with a sour cream base, but I've seen other people making it different ways depending what region of the country they are from. You can feel free and add pecans, walnuts, or even maraschino cherries and bananas like I've seen others do. Mine is refreshing and I use ingredients that I always have on hand. I make it every holiday (per my children's request) or for hot summer barbecues. I am never surprised to find my kids eating spoonful's right out of the bowl. Save some for the rest of us, geez!

MAKES 8 SERVINGS   *Prep time* Less than 5 minutes | *Cooling time* About 1 hour

WHAT YOU'LL NEED

- 1 cup sour cream
- 1 cup mini marshmallows
- 1 cup coconut flakes
- 1 cup pineapple tidbits (well drained)
- 1 cup mandarin oranges (well drained)

LET'S DO THIS!

It really can't get any simpler than this! In a large bowl, add all the ingredients and fold them together.

Refrigerate for 1 hour (or longer, of course, if needed) and serve!

Good for the Soul

There's a reason why this saying sticks—I don't think there is anything more comforting than a bowl of warm soup. Even on your worst days, soup makes things better. It also makes things easier because soup can be done in a blink of an eye. On those chilly nights when I come home from work and I don't have any meal plan, I just open the fridge and my pantry closet, see what I have handy, and throw a few things together that end up being the most delicious soups. I always serve my soups with a nice crusty bread or buttered saltine crackers. Rich and the kids love it! If my girls have friends over, I just add more broth to the pot! That's something my mom always joked around about, but I literally do it. Brothy or hearty, by the spoonful or slurping it up, we don't discriminate! Soup is just so good for the soul!

And I'm sure these simple and fun soups will get your creative juices flowing to come up with your own soup creations in no time!

Tata's Aguadito

My Aunt Tatiana is my mom's baby sister and a true soup lover. She and I have a very close relationship and I remember like it was yesterday the year that she was going to get married. I barely passed school that year because it was like a party every single night, cooking and eating until late. My studies took a back seat to wedding planning! Aguadito was our favorite soup to make, and we had it at least 3 nights a week. It is a traditional Peruvian soup and the word "aguadito" translated literally means "loose." The story goes that it all started when someone was making a traditional chicken and rice dish, and they added too much water! It became loose like a soup. Tata is a pro at it! To this day, every time I take a spoonful it takes me back to all those fun memories. Gosh . . .and thank God I got my shish together and made it through school!

MAKES 8 SERVINGS   *Prep time* 10 minutes | *Cook time* 30 minutes

WHAT YOU'LL NEED

- 8 oz chicken tenderloins cubed and seasoned
- 2 tbsp vegetable oil
- 1 onion, chopped
- 1 medium red bell pepper, sliced
- 2 garlic cloves, chopped
- 2 cups cilantro leaves (purèed with a little water)
- 1 cup carrots, diced
- ½ cup green peas
- 4 cups chicken stock
- ¾ cup long grain rice
- 2 medium yellow potatoes, peeled and cubed

LET'S DO THIS!

Season the chicken with salt and pepper.

In a large pot over high heat, add the chicken pieces and sear them nice and brown.

Transfer the chicken pieces to a plate.

In the same pot, sauté the onions and the garlic.

Add the cilantro puree to the onion mixture.

Add the chicken broth, the bell peppers, and carrots.

Bring it all to a boil, turn the heat to low, cover with a lid, and let it simmer for 10 minutes.

Add the rice, potatoes, and the green peas. Put the lid back on and let it simmer until the potatoes are tender and the rice is cooked—about 20 more minutes.

Remove lid and serve it up!

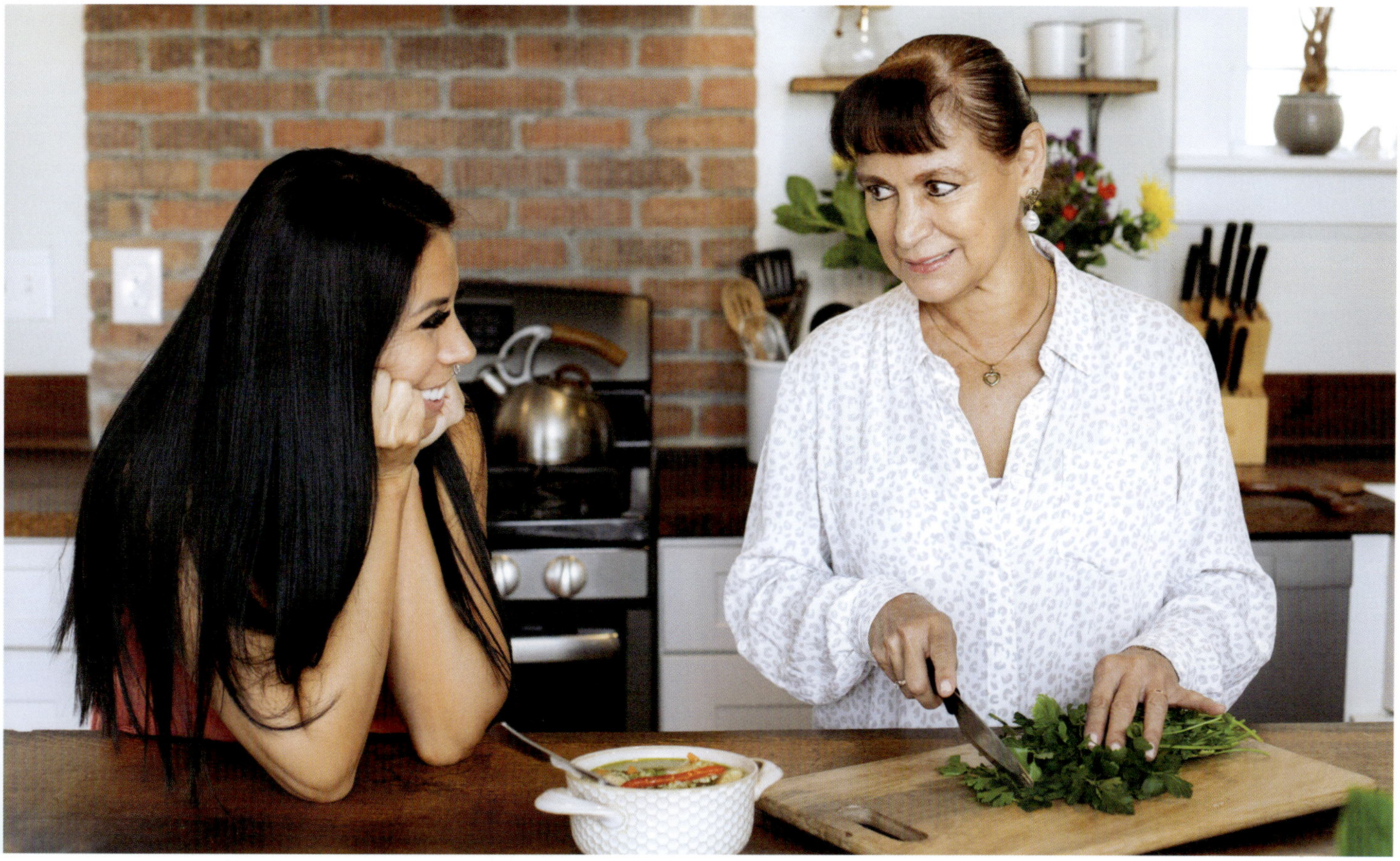

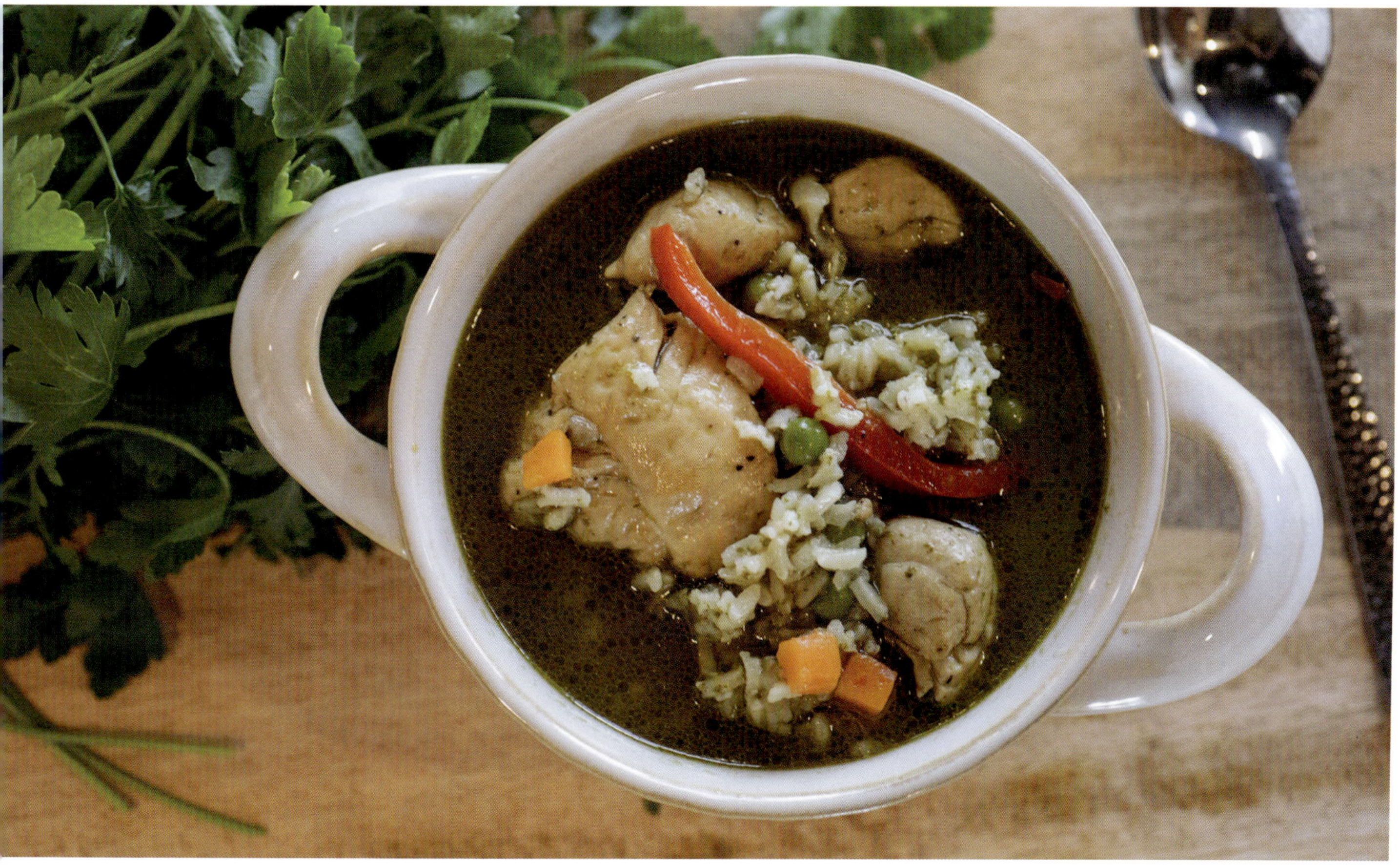

Carla's Take on Chicken Soup

There is something about homemade chicken soup that is so comforting!! It's true. I don't know if it's more the actual soup or the fact that I have memories of my mom making me chicken soup every time I wasn't feeling well. She would always make sure that I'd get all the good nutrients for my body to keep my strength up. I would always hear her saying "you need to feed that cold." My mom makes the best chicken soup, but my children think I make the best chicken soup. I think everybody's mom or dad or grandmother makes the best chicken soup for the same reasons, because it's made with love from whoever is serving it!

In typical Carla fashion, I can never keep a recipe the way it is, I always have to put my own spin on it. With this recipe when I changed it from noodles to little tortellini, it was the best thing I did. It made it fun for my children! They would have races to see who could find the most tortellinis the fastest. Seeing their smiles and making those moments is why I love to cook so much. I like to serve it with some good bread, toast, or simply saltine crackers. There is something about good comfort food that just makes such great memories! I hope when your family thinks of chicken soup they think of you just like I think of my mom and my kids think of me.

MAKES 6 SERVINGS | *Prep time* 10 minutes | *Cook time* 20-25 minutes

WHAT YOU'LL NEED

- 12 oz chicken tenderloin
- 2 tbsp oil
- 1 cup chopped carrots
- 1 cup chopped celery
- 1 cup chopped yellow onions
- 4 garlic cloves, minced
- 6 cups chicken broth
- 12 oz refrigerated three cheese tortellini
- 1 tsp oregano
- salt and pepper to taste

LET'S DO THIS!

In a large pot over medium heat, heat the oil, add the carrots, celery, onions, and sauté for about three to four minutes until soft. Add the garlic and sauté for an extra minute avoid browning.

Add the chicken tenderloin and start to cook. Once they are cooked a little on both sides add the salt, pepper, and the oregano, then pour the chicken broth on top.

Bring everything to a boil for about 15 minutes.

Remove the chicken from this broth and make sure to shred it good! Place it back into the broth and add the tortellini, then cook it uncovered for another 6 to 8 minutes.

Check the seasoning one more time and serve warm.

Chili on a Dime

One of the things my husband grew up on was chili. He comes from a family of four children, and he tells me that his mother always found a way to make meals on a "dollar budget." A good hearty chili is one of his favorite meals. He had high expectations, and I was going to have to make it close to his mother's if I was going to be wife material. I make it my own way, but my husband thinks that it tastes just like his mothers, which makes me very happy because I love to bring those memories back to him always. And we really go old school with this one, because the one thing that can never be missed on the table when we have chili is saltine crackers with butter! I have to call my girls ten minutes before I serve so they can help me butter the crackers and have bowls and bowls of buttered crackers filled up and ready for dipping. My husband doesn't always dip, he likes to scoop a little chili on them and eat them, and my girls like to just dunk the saltines right in the chili. This is something we love to make all the time especially on cold nights

MAKES 6 SERVINGS   *Prep time* 10 minutes | *Cook time* 20 minutes

WHAT YOU'LL NEED

- 2 tbsp vegetable oil
- 1 large onion, chopped
- 3 cloves garlic, finely chopped
- 1 large bell pepper, chopped
- 1 lb ground beef
- 32 oz dark red kidney beans
- 14 ½ oz canned tomato sauce

- 1 ½ cups beef broth
- 1 tbsp chili powder
- 1 tbsp cumin
- ½ tsp black pepper
- salt and pepper to taste
- Optional Garnishes: shredded cheddar cheese, sour cream, corn chips.

LET'S DO THIS!

In a large pot over medium heat, add the oil and cook the onions and bell peppers until they become soft (should be about 3 minutes).Add the garlic and cook for another minute.

Add the beef, breaking it apart with a spatula or a wooden spoon as you cook.Once the beef is partially brown add the spices: cumin, chili powder, salt, and pepper and stir well.

Add the beef broth, tomato sauce, and beans and bring to a quick boil about 1 to 2 minutes stirring occasionally.

Reduce the heat and simmer for about 20 more minutes, allowing all the flavors to develop. Serve the chili with your favorite toppings (and definitely don't forget the crackers!) Serve immediately.

Souper Sunday Pasta e Fagiole

This soup is definitely my personal favorite! It is what I crave on the first cool night of the year. It has the three things that I love the most: meat, beans, and pasta. I love to make it on "Souper Sundays." That's what I call those extra chilly Sundays when I make a big vat of hearty soup for dinner. I top it off with shredded Parmesan cheese and serve it with a big platter of garlic bread on the table. We all love to dip our crusty garlic bread in the soup and this mama can go for seconds or even thirds (no shame on my game)!! I have been making this recipe for as long as I can remember, and the best part is that all the ingredients are always things we keep on hand. It is so so simple and delicious. When life gets busy make Souper Sunday Pasta e Fagiole!

MAKES 6 SERVINGS   *Prep time* 15 minutes | *Cook time* 25 minutes

WHAT YOU'LL NEED

- 2 tbsp olive oil
- 1 lb ground sausage
- 1 large onion chopped
- 1 cup chopped carrots (about 2 medium carrots)
- 1 cup diced celery (about 3 stalks)
- 3 cloves garlic, chopped
- 24 oz tomato sauce
- 4 cups chicken broth
- 1 tsp Italian seasoning
- 1 cup ditalini pasta
- 16 oz red kidney beans, drained
- 16 oz great northern beans, drained
- salt and pepper to taste
- Optional Garnish: grated Parmesan cheese or Romano cheese

LET'S DO THIS!

In a large pot on high heat, add the olive oil, onions, carrots, and celery. Cook well until the vegetables become a little softer.

Add the ground pork and with the help of a spatula or a wooden spoon start to break the meat so it starts to have the ground consistency. Stir occasionally making sure it doesn't brown too much on the bottom.

Add the beans, tomato sauce, chicken broth, salt, pepper, and Italian seasoning.

Bring it to a quick boil and at that point add the pasta!

Once the pasta is almost cooked, reduce to low heat. Let it simmer for about 5 to 10 minutes allowing the flavors to come together.

Serve with grated Parmesan or Romano cheese on top. There is always room to add some yummy garlic bread if you want! I'll never complain about that—just be sure to invite me over if you do!

Lasagna Soup

One of my favorite dishes since I was very little was lasagna. Layers of noodles, creamy ricotta cheese, just enough sauce, and ooh the spices . . . my mouth is watering already! My mother and grandmother would always make it, and even if we went out to an Italian restaurant that would be my top choice off the menu. I make lasagna and lasagna rollups and my family loves it, especially around the holidays. One Sunday when I was about to make my lasagna, I realized the boxes of pasta sheets were broken. I really didn't feel like going back to the store to get more, so I decided to work around it. What can a girl do with broken pasta sheets? Make lasagna soup that's what! This soup became the talk of the night, it was just so tasty. See, never fret with a mishap in the kitchen because it usually leads to something better than you could have come up with on your own! I would have never thought of Lasagna Soup if I didn't have to deal with broken pasta! It literally tastes just like a lasagna but without all the layering and most importantly without all the work! It's done in 20 minutes and is so filling and delicious. I hope you guys love it as much as me and my family.

MAKES 6 SERVINGS **Prep time** 10 minutes | **Cook time** 20 minutes

WHAT YOU'LL NEED

- 2 tbsp olive oil
- 1 medium onion, chopped
- 2 garlic cloves, finely chopped
- 12 oz ground beef
- 1 large can tomato sauce
- 1 large can crushed tomatoes
- 4 to 5 cups beef broth (depending on if you like it thicker or more runny)

- ½ cup heavy cream (I like mine creamy)
- 8 oz shredded mozzarella cheese
- salt, pepper, and Italian seasoning to taste
- ½ box lasagna sheets, broken

LET'S DO THIS!

In a large pot over medium heat, add 2 tablespoons of olive oil, add the onions and the garlic, and stir constantly to avoid browning. I mean constantly!!

Add the ground beef, just make sure with a wooden spoon or spatula you crumble the meat.

Add the salt, pepper, and Italian seasoning.

Add the tomato sauce, the crushed tomatoes, and the beef broth, then bring it to quick boil.

Add the pasta and let it cook per box instructions (usually about 8 to 12 minutes).

Once the pasta is cooked reduce the heat and bring it to a simmer!

Now let's thicken it up. Add the heavy cream, shredded mozzarella, and stir.

Serve with your favorite bread and get ready to lick the bowl!

Throw it Together Taco Soup

This Throw It Together Taco Soup will save your life any night of the week (especially on Taco Tuesdays)!

All you need are a few of these canned ingredients on hand and literally throw them in the pot and let them cook together! Done, delicious, and dinner is served!! Plus, simple as it is you can dress it with so many fun garnishes—like sour cream, guacamole, salsa, jalapeño, extra cheese—you know the standard taco fixins'. It will be done in half an hour, and you can turn any kitchen into a fiesta!

MAKES 8 SERVINGS   *Prep time* 5 minutes | *Cook time* 20 minutes

WHAT YOU'LL NEED

- 2 large cans chicken breast
- 1 medium chopped onion
- 1 small can corn drained
- 1 small can black beans
- 1 small can pinto beans
- 1 small can green chiles
- 1 small can diced tomatoes
- 5 cups chicken broth
- 1 packet taco seasoning
- salt, pepper, and cumin to taste

LET'S DO THIS!

In a large pot over medium heat cook the onions until soft.

Add all the canned ingredients and stir well.

Add all the seasoning and stir again.

Add the chicken broth, bring it to a quick boil, reduce the heat to simmer. Simmer for about 20 minutes allowing all the flavors to come together.

Serve piping hot.

Carla's Tip!

Make it like a real taco party. Garnish with corn chips, tortilla chips, sour cream, shredded cheddar cheese, and diced avocado!

Tasty Tuscan Bean Soup

I have the memory of being in my bedroom and smelling bacon being fried. I would run to the kitchen to see what they were making, and it would always be my mom's famous bacon and bean soup that she made since I was a little girl. This is a little bit of a spin on it! I have switched it a little bit and I adopted an Italian flair. I add either kale or spinach and make it usually with pancetta. But, if the pancetta is not available, I do add sausage or regular old bacon as well. Only a few ingredients make this soup not only easy, but one of the tastiest!! AND it comes in so handy on a very busy weeknight. You know ladies, those hard nights when you're about to pull your hair out and finish the entire bottle of wine. When you need to feed your family with something quick and simple, this soup definitely does the trick, and to top it off it is rather inexpensive. So, it is a winner in all ways.

MAKES 6 SERVINGS   *Prep time* 10 minutes | *Cook time* 20 minutes

WHAT YOU'LL NEED

- 2 tbsp olive oil
- 6 oz ground sausage
  (bacon or pancetta work great too)
- 4 cups chicken broth
- 1 medium yellow onion chopped
- 1 cup chopped carrots
  (about 2 medium carrots)
- ½ cup chopped celery
  (about 1 celery stalk)
- 4 garlic cloves, finely chopped
- 1 tsp Italian seasoning
- 2 cans cannellini beans,
  or great northern beans, drained
- 2 packed cups fresh kale roughly
  chopped (or fresh spinach)
- ½ cup shredded Parmesan cheese
- salt and pepper to taste

LET'S DO THIS!

In a large pot, heat the oil over medium heat, add the onions, carrots, and celery.

Sauté the vegetables until they become softer, then add the chopped garlic and sauté for an extra minute.

Add the ground sausage and cook it with all the vegetables until it starts to become nice and brown.

Add salt, pepper, and Italian seasoning.

Add the chicken broth and the beans.

Lower the heat and cover the pot with the lid, and let it simmer for about 5 minutes.

Add the kale or spinach and stir once more.

Add the Parmesan cheese, and it is ready to serve.

Dinner is Served

What's for dinner? It's probably the most asked question on a daily basis, right mamas? And I'm not going to lie, I have rolled my eyes many times just thinking about it. I feel your pain - you have been working your booty off all day in or outside of the home, on top of that cleaning, doing laundry, doing drop off and pick-ups for school and sports . . . I mean the list goes on! Making dinner might have been on your list earlier, but at this point you are just exhausted to even think about it. And take-out just seems so easy. I've been there, done that!

But I realized that cooking should be quick, not painful, and the moments around the table truly are priceless. To do that, remember these 3 important things: 1) taking shortcuts is okay, 2) using frozen veggies is totally acceptable, and 3) repeating meals doesn't hurt anyone. Make the most out of your leftovers, give yourself some credit and grace, and know you are doing a phenomenal job. Your kiddos won't remember if your dish was garnished properly, but what they will remember is the love you put into making it.

I hope these easy dishes make you look like a Queen, and if you are not your stove's best friend YET, you soon will be! I promise.

Smoky Beef Stir Fry

I love a good beef stir fry! They can be made quick and easy, and they give you a fun, healthier alternative to a carton of take-out Chinese food. I like using beef for my stir fry because it just gives it that extra smoky flavor that a stir fry needs. I usually use a wok to make mine, but if you don't have one, don't sweat it girl! You can easily just use a frying pan. On a busy night or if you are just craving a little Asian food, get your stir fry on! Substitute the beef for your meat of choice and either way this is going to be delicious!

MAKES 6 SERVINGS   *Prep time* 15 minutes | *Cook time* 20 minutes

WHAT YOU'LL NEED

- 2 tbsp vegetable oil
- 1 lb flank steak thinly sliced
- 2 tbsp corn starch
- 4 cups Asian mixed vegetables (the ones I like to use are broccoli, thin sliced carrots, bok choy, red peppers and baby corn)

Sauce

- 3 garlic cloves, minced
- 1 tsp fresh ginger, minced (you can replace with ½ tsp ground ginger)
- ⅓ cup orange juice
- ⅓ cup water
- ¼ cup soy sauce
- 3 tbsp brown sugar
- 2 tsp sesame oil
- 1 tbsp corn starch

LET'S DO THIS!

Season the steak with salt and pepper and toss in the corn starch. Set aside while you prepare the veggies.

Place one tablespoon of oil in a wok. Cook the beef in really hot oil in small batches, to allow the steak to brown and not to boil. This process helps the steak to become nice and smoky. Cook the steak on both sides, remove from the pan, and set aside.

Add the vegetables to the pan and cook for about 2 to 3 minutes because you still want them to be firm and crisp. Remove from the pan and set aside with the beef.

Combine all the sauce ingredients (except for the corn starch) in a bowl and stir really well. Turn the heat up to medium/high. Add the sauce mixture and bring to a simmer.

Combine the corn starch with three tablespoons of water. Add it to the sauce little by little until it starts getting thicker or becomes your desired consistency. Let it simmer for about one minute.

Add the vegetables and the beef and serve over noodles, white rice, or brown rice. Yummy!

Catch Me I'm Falling for Chicken Cacciatore

Yes, I'm in love with this Italian classic! Not only because it's so tasty, but it's simple and doesn't require me to clean a bunch of pots and pans because it all gets done in one!! Plus, it's such a hearty meal. Cacciatore means "hunter" in Italian so when you translate it to this dish it's really all about the rustic hunter-style feel. The most important thing and the tastiest part of this dish is the chicken gets cooked in a lot of sauce to the point it just falls off the bone, because you are going to use chicken thighs to make it nice and flavorful. You can serve it with pasta, polenta, extra vegetables, or roasted potatoes. I like to add a little bit of red pepper flakes because my Latin blood always needs to spice things up.

MAKES 6 SERVINGS | *Prep time* 10 minutes | *Cook time* 40 minutes

WHAT YOU'LL NEED

- 3 tbsp olive oil
- 6 bone-in skinless chicken thighs
- salt and pepper to season
- 1 medium onion, diced
- 6 garlic cloves, minced
- 1 yellow bell pepper, diced
- 1 red bell pepper, diced
- 1 large carrot, peeled and sliced
- 12 oz mushrooms, quartered
- 1 cup red wine
- 24 oz marinara sauce
- ½ tsp red pepper flakes
- 1 tsp dry oregano
- 4 sprigs thyme
- Optional: ½ cup pitted black olives

LET'S DO THIS!

Season the chicken with salt and pepper.

Heat 2 tablespoons of oil in a pot, then sear the chicken on both sides until golden, about 3 to 4 minutes on each side. Remove the chicken and set aside.

Add the remaining tablespoon of oil to the pot, sauté the onions until translucent. Add the garlic and cook for another minute until fragrant. Add the peppers, carrots, mushrooms, and herbs. Cook for about 5 minutes until the vegetables start to soften.

Pour in the wine scraping the browning from the bottom of the pan. Cook until the wine is reduced about two minutes.

Add the marinara sauce and the red pepper flakes. Season with salt and pepper and return the chicken pieces to the pot. Lower the heat all the way to simmer and continue to cook for another 20 to 25 minutes until you see that the chicken is nice and tender, falling off the bone.

Serve with your side of choice. My favorites are pasta, roasted potatoes, or polenta!

Chicken Enchilada Casserole

You know, when you love something so much, you want it all the time, and then eventually you get sick of it? Well, that was my worry with this dish, that my family would get tired of it and this casserole is definitely too good for that. The first time I made this casserole it instantly became a favorite in my house. It would be a dinner request week after week, sometimes even twice a week, and there was actually a point where I had to cut my family off from it for a little bit. After a nice little detox from it, now I just surprise them with it every once in a while depending on their behavior. Like the majority of my recipes, this one is really easy to make. It is a great dish for potlucks, entertaining guests or just to have on a busy weeknight. When it comes to the cheese you know how I feel: the more the merrier! So, load up and enjoy!

MAKES 6-8 SERVINGS   *Prep time* 10 minutes | *Cook time* 30 minutes

WHAT YOU'LL NEED

- 8 small flour tortillas, cut into halves

- 2 cups cooked shredded chicken (rotisserie chicken works great for this recipe)

- 2 cups shredded jack cheese, or Mexican cheese

- 1 can black beans or pinto beans, rinsed and drained

- 2 cups red enchilada sauce (usually comes in a can)

- cooking spray

- Optional Garnishes: sour cream, green onions, avocado, diced tomatoes, sliced black olives

LET'S DO THIS!

Preheat the oven to 350°F.

Coat an 8x8 oven proof baking dish with cooking spray.

Spread ¼ cup of the enchilada sauce on the bottom of the baking dish.

Layer 4 halves of the tortillas over the sauce, covering the bottom of the pan.

Layer ⅓ of the chicken, one third of the beans, half a cup of the cheese, and one third of the enchilada sauce over the tortillas.

Place a second layer of tortillas over the top of the chicken. Then blend and layer once again a third of the chicken, a third of the beans, half a cup of the cheese, and ⅓ cup of the enchilada sauce. Repeat this process one more time for a third layer. You got this!

Place the remaining tortilla pieces over the top and spread the rest of the enchilada sauce over the tortillas, then sprinkle the remaining cheese over the top.

Cover with foil and cook for about 20 minutes. Then uncover it and cook 10 more minutes until the cheese
on top is melted and starts to brown.

Let it sit for about 5 to 10 minutes so it comes together and firms up, then serve with whatever toppings you prefer!

Spiced Soda Pulled Pork

I make this pulled pork in the crockpot, and you might be asking why I'm using spiced soda. First off, if you don't have a spiced soda, don't sweat it girl, you can always use cola, but the spiciness gives it a little extra flavor combined with the pork. Actually, the soda is what helps tenderize the meat making it melt in your mouth. When the pork simmers slowly with the soda paired with the blend of spices it gives an explosion of flavor. I never thought I'd be suggesting for people to use soda to cook with, but I'm telling you it's only one can and it makes all the difference. I love serving this dish when I have to feed a lot of people. I can put it in the crockpot and totally forget about it. I use this for my famous sheet pan nachos and if I'm entertaining, I use this pulled pork for sandwiches or tacos. It is so versatile, and it never fails me, and if I make enough of it, I can get more than one meal out of it for the week. It simplifies my life for a few days!! Jackpot. Who doesn't love that, right?

MAKES 8 SERVINGS   *Prep time* 5 minutes | *Cook time* 4 hours

WHAT YOU'LL NEED

- 1 pork butt/pork shoulder roast (about 4 to 5 lbs)

- salt, pepper, and garlic powder to taste

- 1 can spiced soda

- 1 cup barbeque sauce (have more on hand if you like extra saucy, like me!)

- Optional: 1 yellow onion sliced

LET'S DO THIS!

Rub the outside of the roast with salt, pepper, and garlic powder. If you are going to add the onions, then you should place them on the bottom of the slow cooker right now.

Add the roast to the slow cooker and pour the spiced soda over the pork. Cook on high for 4 to 5 hours or on low for 7 to 8 hours (the time length is up to you, on when you will need it ready by).

Once the meat is ready it will be very tender, like melt in your mouth tender. Using two forks shred the pork and add back into the juices.

Add barbeque sauce to taste, 1 cup is usually good, but I like mine extra saucy!

Allow to cook an extra 20 minutes, but you can serve it right away after adding the sauce if you desire.

Nice 'n Crisp Eggplant Parmigiana

This was a dish on the top of my list that I wanted to master when I was still a pescatarian. The area that I live in is full of Italian restaurants, so when I would go out to eat dinner at any of them my choices would be limited. Eggplant parm was, by default, the dish I had to choose off the menu. I had never tried one that really spoke to my foodie heart, so I made it my goal to come up with my own. Well, if I'm determined enough to do something, I always figure out a way. So, are you ready to hear the three secrets for the best eggplant parm?

First, the eggplant needs to be sliced very thin, so it doesn't become soggy while you bake it off. Second, keep a bowl of water and ice nice and close to your cutting board because as you are slicing up the eggplant, you will want to place the slices into an ice bath to prevent them from browning, and this also takes the bitterness out. Last but not least, the final secret is that you mix the flour with the breadcrumbs for a thicker and crunchier crust. So, girl, the secret is out!! These tricks make it next level awesome, and once you've had it like this, you will never want to order out eggplant parm again!

MAKES 6 SERVINGS   *Prep time* 30 minutes | *Cook time* 30 minutes

WHAT YOU'LL NEED

- 2 medium eggplants, cut into ¼ inch round slices

- 4 cups breadcrumbs

- 2 cups all-purpose flour

- 6 large eggs, beaten

- 1 lb shredded mozzarella cheese

- 1 cup grated Parmesan cheese

- 6 cups marinara sauce ½ cup fresh basil, julienne

- 1 tbsp dry oregano

- 1 tbsp dry basil

- 1 tbsp paprika

- ground black pepper

- salt

- vegetable oil for frying

LET'S DO THIS!

Peel the eggplant and cut it into quarter inch round slices.

Prepare a bowl with water and ice to make an ice bath. As you cut the slices of eggplant make sure they are submerged in the ice water. This takes away the bitter juices and helps make a nice crisp eggplant.

Leave the slices in the water for at least 10 minutes. Remove the slices and pat dry with paper towels.

In a large bowl, whisk the breadcrumbs, flour, oregano, basil, paprika, and season with salt and pepper.

In another large bowl, beat the eggs.

Pass the eggplant through the egg mixture and right after through the breadcrumb mixture so the egg mixture can absorb a good coating of the breadcrumb mixture and set them aside on a sheet pan.

After you have each piece ready with the breading, heat a sauté pan or skillet with oil. Make sure that it is hot. Fry each piece of eggplant browning them until on both sides.

As you remove the eggplant from the frying pan, place them on a plate with paper towel so the excess oil can be absorbed. Work through batches until you finish frying off!

Preheat your oven to 375°F.

On an oven proof baking dish (9 x 13 or 10 x 15 works great), pour a ladle of marinara sauce over the bottom of the dish, place a layer of the eggplant over the sauce, add some of the fresh julienne basil and mozzarella cheese.

Repeat the steps with another layer of sauce and eggplant. Cover the eggplant with more sauce and mozzarella cheese, top it off with the Parmesan cheese. Cover it with aluminum foil and bake it off for 20 minutes. Remove the aluminum foil for the last 10 minutes allowing the cheese to brown on top.

Let it sit for about 5 to 10 minutes so it comes together and firms up, then serve with whatever toppings you prefer!

Hot Honey Chicken

Do you know which is one of my favorite cities? Nashville, Tennessee - Music City baby! It just makes me so happy. I go there very often, and I'm really a country girl at heart. I enjoy going to every single honky-tonk and stomping my boots to a good old country song. And of course, I never leave without having a hot chicken sandwich. I always make it my first stop–a hot chicken sandwich and fried pickles. This Hot Honey Chicken is a creation of mine that came from my love for the hot honey we produce at the farm and the famous Nashville hot chicken sandwich. It is actually made in the oven, so you don't have to deal with all the splashing of oil and grease but is still just as tasty. When we have this at home the one thing that always happens without fail, is as soon as we take the first bite everyone around the table looks at each other to see who is going to be the first one to start tearing up from the heat. If you're a lover of hot food make sure you add this recipe to your menu. Don't worry, I won't tell anyone I saw you cry.

MAKES 4 SERVINGS   *Prep time* 15 minutes | *Cook time* 35-40 minutes

WHAT YOU'LL NEED

- 1 lb chicken tenderloin
- 1 cup buttermilk
- 2 tbsp flour
- 2 cups super fine breadcrumbs
- salt, pepper, and paprika to taste

Coating

- 1 cup hot honey
- 1 tbsp paprika
- ½ cup vegetable oil
- 1 tsp garlic powder
- 1 tsp cayenne pepper
- 3 tbsp white vinegar
- salt and pepper to taste

LET'S DO THIS!

Place all your chicken tenderloins in a sandwich bag or container with the buttermilk and let them sit for about 5 minutes. Preheat the oven to 400°F.

In a deep dish or bowl mix your breadcrumbs, flour, salt, pepper, and paprika. Set aside.

Remove all the chicken from the buttermilk and place them in the breadcrumb mixture one by one, making sure they are coated entirely. Place them all on a baking sheet lined with parchment paper, leaving space between each chicken tenderloin.

Drizzle a little olive oil over each chicken tenderloin to allow them to bake off. Place in the oven for 30 to 35 minutes until cooked through and nice 'n crispy!

Make the sauce by combining the honey, paprika, vegetable oil, garlic powder, cayenne pepper, white vinegar, salt, and pepper. Mix very well and add it to saucepan to warm it up. You can use the sauce to brush on top, for dipping, or just simply pour it right over the top!

Tacu Tacu a lo Pobre

Tacu Tacu is an authentic Peruvian dish made out of the leftover rice and beans. These days you can find it on almost every menu in a Peruvian restaurant, but growing up I remember my father and brother having it for breakfast! While I was having yogurt and fresh juice, they would be eating Tacu Tacu right in front of my face. (How lucky they are with their fast metabolisms!) Ok let me stop hating on them and get back to the dish. The term "A lo pobre" is pretty sarcastic because it literally means "the poor way", but there is nothing poor about having a fried steak, fried bananas, and fried egg on top. For me the best part about this dish is the memories it brings back of sitting around the table with my dad and brother while they were laughing and joking at me about the new diet I was on while they were enjoying Tacu Tacu. Use this dish to add a little Peruvian flair to your dinner table, but don't forget to make enough to have leftovers for breakfast!

MAKES 4 SERVINGS   *Prep time* 10 minutes | *Cook time* 30 minutes

WHAT YOU'LL NEED

- 2 cups leftover rice cooked
- 4 large frying bananas, peeled
- 4 eggs
- 4 cuts of steak of your choice

For the Beans

- 3 tbsp olive oil
- 1 medium yellow onion, chopped
- 3 garlic cloves, minced
- 2 cans cannellini beans
- salt and pepper to taste
- 1 tbsp of aji amarillo paste

For the Salsa Criolla

- 2 red onions, thinly sliced
- juice of one lime
- 1 tbsp white vinegar
- ½ tsp chile peppers finely chopped
- salt and pepper to taste

LET'S DO THIS!

In a pot, heat the oil and add the onions until they become soft. Add the minced garlic and cook for an extra minute. Add the aji amarillo paste. Stir for an extra 30 seconds

Add the drained beans and stir them in the pot. Season with salt and pepper and let it simmer and thicken. Set aside.

Mix the rice and the beans and divide into four portions. Make the rice and beans like a cake and fry it on one side. Allow it to brown and then flip.

Fry banana halves in oil until golden brown.

Prepare your steaks with salt and pepper and fry them to your desired temperature.

Serve the rice and bean patties with the fried banana and steak on top and at the very last minute add a fried egg over everything!

Firecracker Shrimp

The first time I tried Firecracker Shrimp was as an appetizer at a seafood restaurant. Right away I was in love! It had the perfect amount of heat, the sauce was smooth and delicious, and the shrimp itself was incredibly done. By the time I had left the restaurant my taste buds were having a happy dance and my brain was trying to figure out all the ingredients in that dish. I know, you might be thinking, "Carla turn your brain off and just enjoy the food!" But then I wouldn't be writing this cookbook and you wouldn't be making this deliciousness, so I'll just keep my brain going.

Even though I had no idea of the exact ingredients or measurements, I wasn't going to stop until I could recreate this recipe. The very next day I went to the store, got my ingredients, came home, put my apron on, and cranked up the Rocky Balboa song. I was ready for the challenge, and I nailed it! (I promise you, I'm not bragging; it was just a very proud moment.) I will make this dish as an appetizer or for dinner, on top of a rice bowl or with some vegetables. No matter how it is served, I've never seen any leftover!

MAKES 6 SERVINGS *Prep time* Less than 10 minutes | *Cooking time* Less than 10 minutes

WHAT YOU'LL NEED

Shrimp

- 1 lb medium shrimp, peeled and deveined
- ½ cup corn starch
- 2 large eggs
- ¼ cup vegetable or canola oil
- ¼ cup sliced green onions
- salt and pepper to taste

Sauce

- ½ cup sweet chili garlic sauce
- 3 tbsp fresh squeezed lemon juice
- 3 tbsp honey
- 1 tbsp lemon zest
- 1 tsp sriracha sauce
- ½ tsp ground ginger
- ½ tsp ground garlic
- salt and pepper to taste

LET'S DO THIS!

In a large saucepan over medium/high heat, heat the oil.

In a large bowl, season the shrimp with salt and pepper, and lightly toss the shrimp in corn starch until coated (sometimes I like to put the shrimp in a sandwich bag so I can shake it and make sure it is well coated with the corn starch evenly).

Dip the shrimp individually into the beaten eggs right before you are about to drop them into the frying pan.

Add the shrimp little by little to the pan, but don't over-add so they can be cooked well and be golden brown on both sides. As they finish remove and place on a plate with paper towel, repeat the process with all the shrimp until finished.

In a different pan, combine the sweet chili garlic sauce, lemon juice, honey, lemon zest, sriracha, ground ginger, garlic, salt, and pepper bring to a quick boil for about two minutes. Let it reduce slightly and add the shrimp! Make sure they are coated well garnish with the sliced green onions and serve immediately.

Blue Ribbon Turkey Meatloaf

I'm proud to say, this actually is an award-winning recipe! Might only be at my friends Guy and Donna's house, but still it is first prize in my eyes. Let me go more into detail. My friends Guy and Donna always love to host parties, but they always have to have a theme. We have teamed up to make pasta, fresh mozzarella, and we have even had cook offs. This time it was a meatloaf cookoff where everyone had to bring their best recipe and put it to the test. I already felt pressure for trying to have the best meatloaf for that cook off, and of course my husband had to add to it by saying. "Hon, you need to really show off. Hon, we have to win this contest." Thanks Rich! I will say though he is a great cheerleader and was there for moral support the whole way through. When it came time to choose the winner, all the husbands took on the role of being the judges. I was anxiously watching everybody's face as they were taking bites, crossing my fingers and praying that they would love mine the most. After I saw the reactions on the husbands' faces when they tried mine, I knew right away that I was going to be the winner. When they announced the winning meatloaf, Rich proudly yelled, "Yay, I won!" Of course, I knew deep down I was going to win, but I had to stay very humble about it. It was a night filled with lots of laughs and meatloaf of all kinds, but in the end the turkey meatloaf took the award and got the bragging rights amongst all the other wives.

Prep time 5 minutes | *Cook time* 50-55 minutes

WHAT YOU'LL NEED

- 1 ½ lbs ground turkey
- 1 cup white onions, chopped
- 4 garlic cloves, minced
- 1 cup seasoned breadcrumbs
- 2 eggs
- 3 tsp Worcestershire sauce

- 2 tbsp freshly chopped parsley
- 1 tsp salt
- ½ tsp black pepper
- 1 tbsp paprika
- 2 tbsp olive oil

Gravy

- 1 cup chicken broth
- ½ tsp garlic powder
- ½ tsp onion powder
- 1 tsp brown gravy helper

- 2 tbsp corn starch
  (diluted in one tbsp cold water)
- fresh thyme sprig

LET'S DO THIS!

In a skillet add the olive oil, onion and the garlic and cook them fully, allow them to cool.

In the meantime, in a bowl combine the turkey, breadcrumbs, egg, Worcestershire sauce, parsley, salt, pepper, paprika, and the onion mixture. Mix everything together well.

In an 8 x 4 inch loaf pan (I usually use a non-stick loaf pan, but if you don't have one make sure you put aluminum foil inside the pan before adding the mixture). Add the turkey mixture to the pan and drop the pan with the mixture in it from a few inches above the table or counter allowing the mixture to tighten up preventing any air gaps.

Bake at 350°F for about 50 to 55 minutes, the internal temperature should be 165°F. Remove from the oven and let it stand.

Remove the meatloaf from the pan and save those turkey drippings.

To make the gravy, add one cup of chicken broth to all the drippings of the turkey meatloaf. Let it reduce for a little bit. Add the garlic powder, onion powder, salt and pepper and thyme and let it reduce. Add the brown gravy helper and corn starch, mix it until it thickens, pour on top of the meatloaf and get ready to lick the plate!

Schnitzel Italiano

This is basically an original German schnitzel with Parmesan cheese (which technically makes it more of a Pork Chop Milanese), but the schnitzel is something that reminds me of my brother, so Schnitzel Italiano it is! A lot of people might not know, but my brother and I grew up going to a German school in Peru. My dad always liked a strict structure and wanted us to be well educated and bilingual. After finishing school my brother headed out to live in Germany. One of my best memories is the time I had an impromptu visit with him. I called him on a Monday and was in Germany by the Thursday. He canceled all his plans, and we had the most amazing weekend together. Even though the trip was very last minute, my brother made plans to travel to the city of Ruedeshheim. He said it was a "must-see" because of the gorgeous views, the farm style living, and the quaint atmosphere. He knows me well and knows what I love!

In the rush of the last-minute planning, he forgot to take into consideration that the restaurants stop serving food between lunch and dinner. When we got there, we just missed the lunch rush and had to wait until dinner was able to be served. So, what did we do for three hours while we waited? We drank! Beer after beer after beer. When it was finally time to be served, the first thing I wanted was a pork schnitzel. I devoured that schnitzel in record time (and I am known to be a fast eater). I'm not even sure if it's the best schnitzel I've ever had in my life or if it was just the beer talking, but for sure it is one of the most amazing memories I've ever had with my brother!

When I make this dish, I think of sitting in the quaint German countryside with my brother eating schnitzel. I can still see the look he was giving me while I was stuffing my face (he is much more sophisticated than I am).

MAKES 4 SERVINGS   *Prep time* 15 minutes | *Cook time* 10 minutes

WHAT YOU'LL NEED

- 4 boneless pork loin chops

- 1 cup mayonnaise

- 2 cups seasoned panko breadcrumbs

- ⅓ cup parmesan cheese

- olive oil or vegetable oil to fry

LET'S DO THIS!

Using a meat tenderizer pound the pork chop a little bit, until they become about a half an inch thick. You want them to all be even in thickness.

Put the mayonnaise in a bowl and pass the pork chop through it, giving it a good coat of mayo.

In a separate bowl, combine the seasoned panko breadcrumbs with the parmesan cheese.

Press each piece of the mayo coated pork chops into the breadcrumb mix, pressing gently so a good layer of the breadcrumb mix adheres to the pork.

Heat about 4 tablespoons of oil in a large skillet over medium heat. Once it's hot, add the pork chops. This may need to be done in smaller batches to allow proper browning on both sides. Cook for about 3 to 4 minutes each side, until golden brown and crispy. The internal temperature will be about 145°F!

Remove the pork and let it rest a few minutes before serving. It was a lot of work to get it to taste this good so it needs a break. ☺

You can serve it with your favorite side dish. I usually like to have it with a little arugula salad.

Sunday Cheats

I've never met a pasta I didn't like . . . or wine! I think I was 10000% Italian in my past life because pasta is my weakness and wine is my favorite. My family and close friends know that I start a new diet every Monday, but by lunch time I'm trying to break it, and by dinner time it's game over. (I blame it on the wine). I honestly try to watch what I eat (for the most part) during the week, but as soon as Sunday comes, my mouth starts watering just thinking of the pasta dish I will make at night. In our house Sunday is not just a regular day of the week, for us, it's Pasta Sunday! It's so much fun having my girls around the kitchen island helping me cook, Rich pouring the wine, and Alex playing with the spaghetti!

If you guys want to be cheaters ... cheat with pasta! No shame on my game. ☺ I don't think I have one favorite recipe ... I love them all!

Grab your glass of wine, get your pasta cooking, and join the Sunday Cheating Club.

Homemade Beefaroni

A bowl of this pasta will make you feel like a kid again! This dish definitely takes the prize for the best comfort food. It takes minimal ingredients and it's ready in less than 30 minutes. Yay! Now that's my kind of dinner! The perfect dish for a Sunday meal to gather around the table with your loved ones or works great as a quick weeknight meal for all you busy mamas. If your kids like the canned version, they are going to love this homemade one ten times more, and they will be thinking you are Chef Boyar-mama in no time!

MAKES 6-8 SERVINGS   *Prep time* 5 minutes | *Cook time* 20 minutes

WHAT YOU'LL NEED

- 1 lb ground beef

- 1 medium yellow onion, chopped

- 4 garlic cloves, minced

- 1 tsp Italian seasoning

- 24 oz marinara sauce (store bought or homemade)

- 1 lb elbow macaroni

- 1 cup shredded Parmesan cheese

- salt and pepper to taste

LET'S DO THIS!

Cook the elbow macaroni according to the instructions on the package.

In a large pot over medium heat, cook the onions until soft, add the garlic and stir 1 more minute.

Add the ground beef with the Italian seasoning, salt and pepper, making sure the beef is fully cooked.

Stir in the marinara sauce and simmer on low for about 10 to 12 minutes.

Stir in the elbow macaroni, add the shredded Parmesan cheese, mix well and serve!

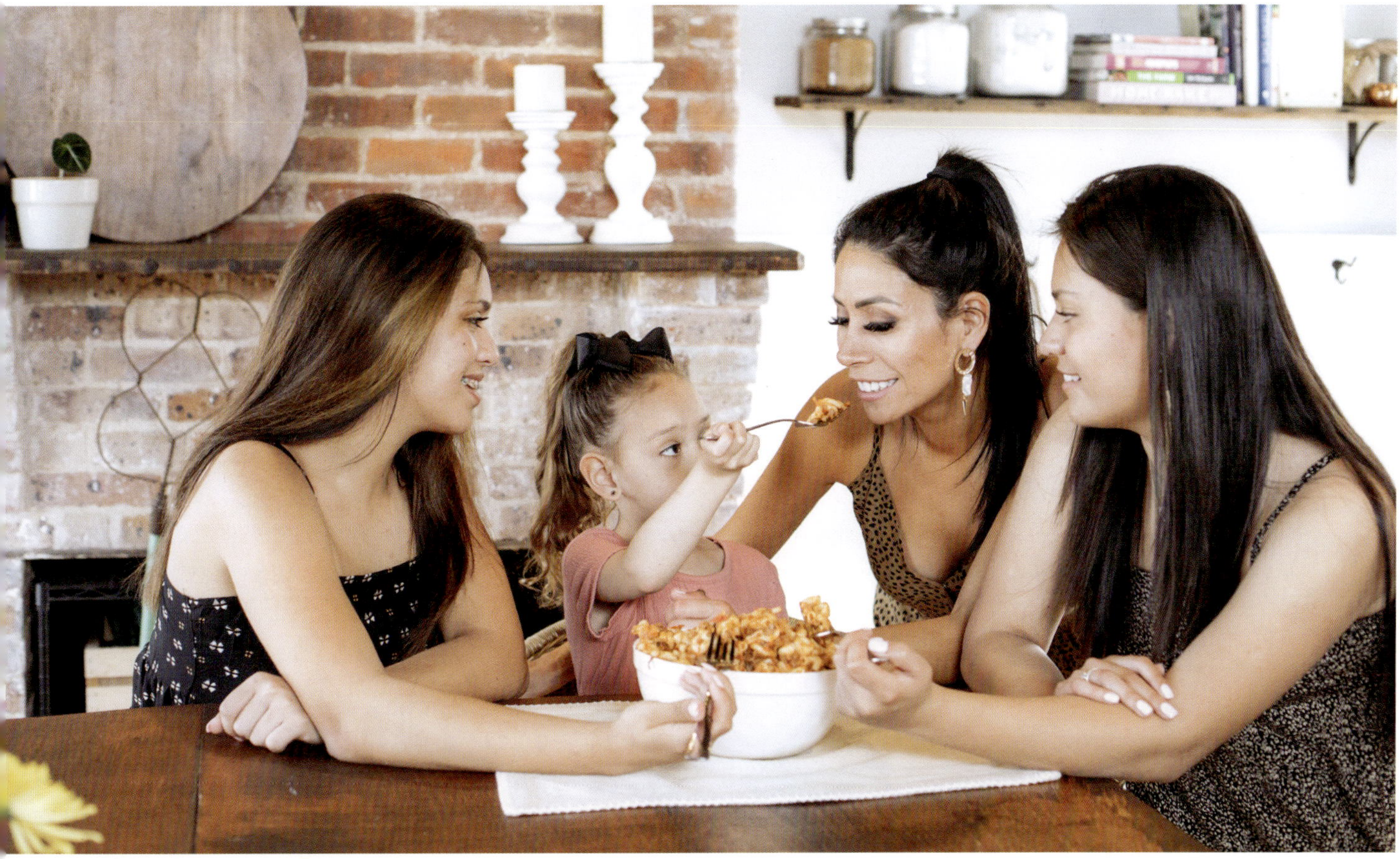

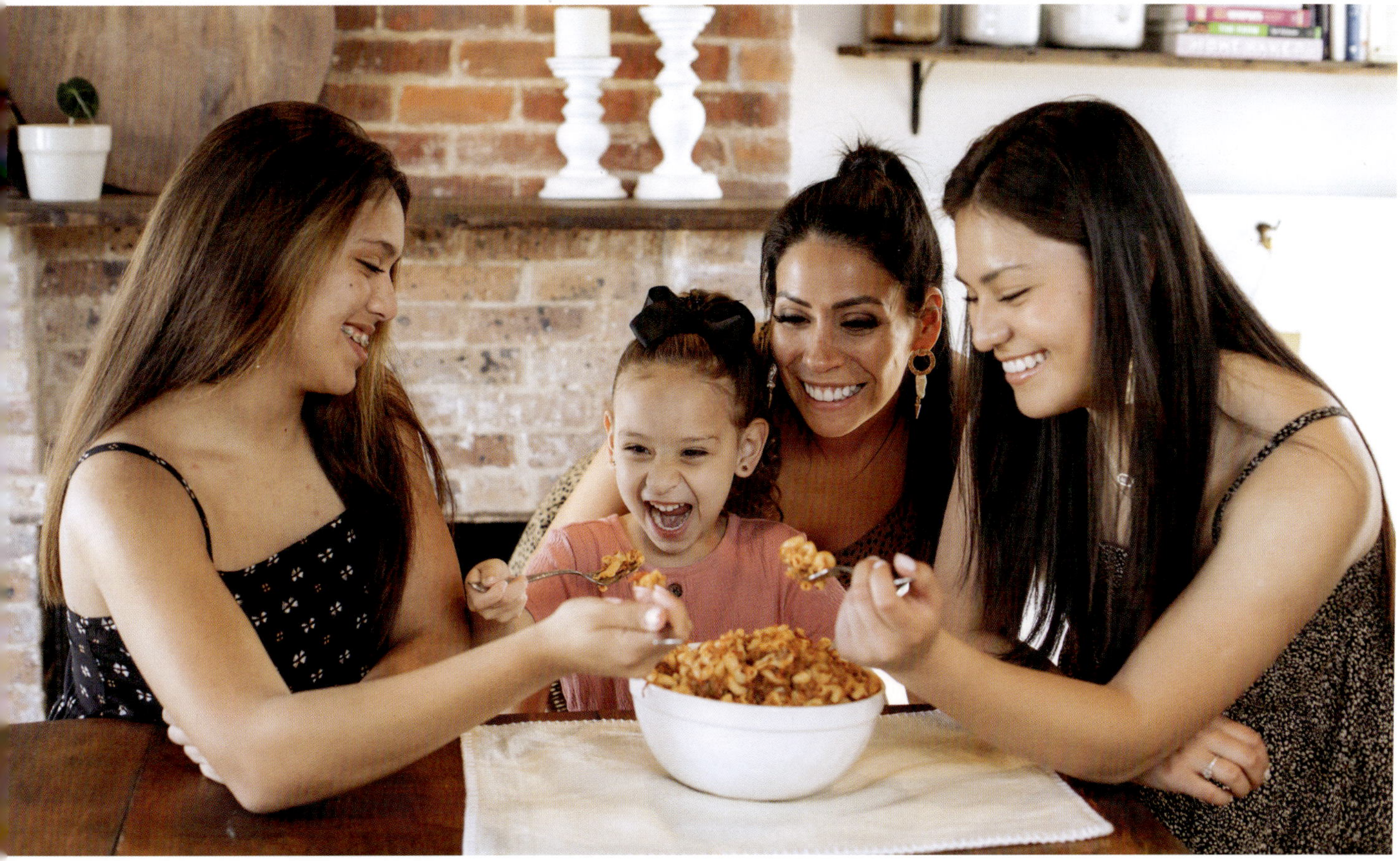

Pop a Button Carbonara

If you've had carbonara before, I want to warn you–this is NOT your traditional Roman carbonara that only uses eggs as a binding component. I actually add heavy cream to mine (if you are true Italian, please don't kill me!). I just love it being extra creamy and in case you haven't noticed, I always have to twist recipes to make them my own. I ate so much pasta carbonara when I was in Italy that when I came home none of my pants would fit, but hey, isn't it the memories that count? So, get your stretchy pants on and enjoy.

MAKES 6 SERVINGS   *Prep time* 5 minutes | *Cook time* 20 minutes

WHAT YOU'LL NEED

- 1 box pasta
- 10 slices thick cut bacon, diced small
- 1 medium onion, finely chopped
- 4 garlic cloves, minced
- 2 whole eggs
- 2 egg yolks
- 1 cup grated Parmesan cheese
- 1 cup heavy cream
- salt and pepper to taste

LET'S DO THIS!

Cook the pasta according to the package directions.

While the pasta is cooking, fry the bacon in the pan, just barely until crisp.

Remove the bacon from the pan and pour off the bacon grease but do not clean the pan. You need that fat for flavor!

Return the pan to the stove and over medium heat cook the onion and the garlic until golden brown, remove from heat and then set aside.

In a bowl mix together the eggs, egg yolks, grated Parmesan cheese, cream, and the salt and pepper. Mix until smooth.

Little by little, add the egg mixture over the cooked onions in the pan, not on the stove.

When the pasta is done, reserve a cup or two of the pasta water. Drain the pasta and place in a bowl.

Bring the egg mixture back onto the heat and whisk it quickly just to warm it up but avoid making it scrambled eggs.

Add the pasta to it mixing it well. Add the pasta water to it as needed, making it creamier

Bring the bacon back into the mixture, stir until combined and serve immediately.

Linguine with Clam Sauce for Soph

When my oldest daughter Sophia was around six years old, she came to me frowning one night after I made this beautiful chicken dish. She said, "Chicken again! I hate chicken!" My patience was short, and sarcastically I asked, "What would *you* like to eat honey?" To which she replied, "Lobster, crab legs, maybe clams." When she said that I couldn't do anything but laugh. My wallet heard clams, that's all I could really afford at the time from her choices. To this day that kid is still a complete seafood lover. Every time I make pasta she is always asking if it is with clam sauce. So, this dish is for my Sophia and the seafood lover in you.

MAKES 6 SERVINGS   *Prep time* 5 minutes | *Cook time* 20 minutes

WHAT YOU'LL NEED

- 1 box linguine
- 3 tbsp olive oil
- 1 medium onion, chopped
- 4 garlic cloves, finely chopped
- ¾ cup dry white wine
- 24 oz marinara sauce
- 2 lbs littleneck clams (about 25)
- ¼ cup fresh chopped parsley
- ½ tsp red pepper flakes
- ¼ tsp Old Bay seasoning
- salt and pepper to taste

LET'S DO THIS!

Bring a large pot of salted water to a boil, add the pasta and cook according to the label instructions. Drain the pasta and set aside.

In a large pot over medium heat, add the olive oil, add the chopped onions cooking until soft, add the garlic and cook for an extra minute avoiding browning.

Add the Old Bay seasoning, red pepper flakes, salt, and pepper.

Add the wine and cook until it reduces by half, about 2 more minutes.

Add the marinara sauce and stir occasionally for another 2 minutes.

Add all of the clams (previously washed). The clams will be ready when they are fully opened, if some of the clams don't open that means they were no good and throw them away. After adding the clams, cover the pot and check in about three to four minutes to see how they are opening. If they need a little more time, continue cooking for another 2 to 3 minutes more.

Add the pasta to the sauce, add the fresh parsley and toss to combine. Then it's ready to serve!

No Time for Shells Taco Pasta

I am known for being a little unruly (okay maybe a lot unruly, depending on the day) and that definitely doesn't change when it comes to food. I remember one time when someone told me that I couldn't have red wine if I was going to have fish for my main course. I feel like people should be free to do whatever makes their hearts happy! And that's the life motto I follow - you do you and do what makes you happy. So, my answer was: "Why not, who makes the rules?" I make my own rules and when it comes to food. I eat whatever I feel like (sorry guys it's my feisty Spanish blood). Now you might be thinking tacos and pasta do NOT go together. Well let me tell you, all I can say is I'm surprised nobody had thought of this sooner because it brings delicious to a whole new level. When I created this recipe, I had full intentions of making tacos, but I was missing the shells. When all else fails I always rely on my trusty go-to: pasta. As usual it never lets me down, so girlfriend make some No Time for Shells Taco Pasta, pour a glass of red wine, and explore your unruly side! And by the way, improvising always makes the BEST new takes on classics!!

MAKES 6 SERVINGS   *Prep time* 10 minutes | *Cook time* 15 minutes

WHAT YOU'LL NEED

- 1 lb ground beef

- 2 tbsp vegetable oil

- 1 medium yellow onion, diced

- 4 garlic cloves, minced

- 1 can tomato sauce

- 1 small can kernelled corn, drained

- 1 small can green chilis, drained

- 1 cup shredded Mexican cheese, or jack cheese

- 1 packet taco seasoning

- salt and pepper

- 1 package pasta your choice (I usually like a short pasta for this, shells, elbow macaroni, or rotini)

- 1 tbsp fresh cilantro, chopped

- 1 cup sour cream

LET'S DO THIS!

In a large skillet over medium/high heat add the onions. Cook until soft, then add the garlic and cook for an additional minute.

Add the ground beef cooking it through, breaking it apart to make it crumble.

Add the taco seasoning.

In a different pot, cook the pasta per instructions and rinse and drain after finished.

Once the beef is done add the salt, pepper, tomato sauce, corn, and green chilis and bring it to a simmer!

Add the cup of sour cream and stir well. Add the pasta, shredded cheese, cilantro combine well and serve! It's easy peasy and oh so good!

Fabulous 15-Minute Pasta

I can make a pasta dish in 15 minutes. "Don't believe me, just watch!" (Thank you, Bruno Mars!!) Seriously, if I can make it, I have no doubt that you can make it too! You can make the sauce while the pasta cooks, and you will most definitely please the crowd because this dish is off the hook!!

MAKES 6 SERVINGS · *Prep time* 5 minutes | *Cook time* 10 minutes

WHAT YOU'LL NEED

- 1 box pasta your choice
- 3 tbsp olive oil
- 8 oz sweet Italian sausage
- 4 garlic cloves, minced
- ½ cup cherry tomatoes, cut in half
- 2 cups fresh spinach
- ½ cup white wine
- 2 cups chicken broth
- 2 tbsp flour
- ½ cup grated Parmesan cheese
- salt and pepper to taste
- Optional: red pepper flakes

LET'S DO THIS!

Cook the pasta per box instructions.

In a large pot over medium heat, add the olive oil.

Add the ground sausage and break it up with a wooden spoon, then add the fresh minced garlic, salt, pepper, and red pepper flakes (if desired) and stir. Cook until it starts browning.

Add the white wine, letting it reduce to half. At this time add the flour and make sure you mix it well so it doesn't become clumpy.

Add the chicken broth—the flour will allow it to thicken nice.

Add the spinach and stir. Add the cherry tomatoes at the end.

Once the sauce is nice and thick add the pasta all in, toss it, add the grated Parmesan cheese and serve.

Sidekicks

Every great superhero needs a trusty sidekick, and a delicious dinner entree is no exception. After all, what is a good steak without the potatoes? A great side can make it or break it, so don't underestimate the power of an average potato or something as simple as some sweet corn, because with a little love and attention they will outshine the finest cuts of meat. Okay, maybe that is an exaggeration, but they definitely can take a meal that is a 7 and turn it into a 10!

Let me introduce you to
the BEST sidekicks in town. .

My Sweetie's Sweet Potato Casserole

I get up very early on Thanksgiving to start my cooking. The girls start waking up as soon as they smell the pancetta and the vegetables being cooked for the stuffing. I would start seeing their pretty faces come and say, "Happy Thanksgiving, Mommy!" They grab their coffee and come join me around the kitchen island and we start to talk and laugh while we cook. Sophia's designated dish is this candied sweet potato casserole. She makes it to perfection, and it is literally her Thanksgiving meal. I actually save my portion for dessert time because it is just so sweet. Side dish or dessert that will be your choice, but either way you won't be disappointed! Oh, and by the way, this is a staple on our Thanksgiving dinner, but we also make it when we have roasted chicken or ham. It is just so delicious!

MAKES 6-8 SERVINGS   *Prep time* 10 minutes | *Cook time* 40 minutes

WHAT YOU'LL NEED

- 6 large sweet potatoes, peeled and sliced about ½ an inch thick

- 1 cup unsalted butter

- 1 ½ cups brown sugar, packed

- ⅛ tsp salt

- 2 tsp ground cinnamon

- 1 tsp ground nutmeg

- ½ tsp ground ginger

- 4 cups mini marshmallows

- 1 cup heavy cream

LET'S DO THIS!

Preheat the oven to 375°F. Place the potato slices in a pot, fill the pot with water until the water covers the potatoes, and put them to boil until the potatoes become soft.

Drain the potatoes using a colander. In a bowl, smash the sweet potatoes until smooth, add the melted butter, heavy cream, brown sugar, salt, cinnamon, nutmeg, and ginger.

Add this mixture to a 9 x 13 baking dish and top it with marshmallows. Cook for 10 to 15 minutes until the marshmallows start to become golden. If you need to you can broil the marshmallows a little bit— it gives it great texture and even better flavor!

Easy Peasy Corn Pudding

This is my American version on my grandma's traditional corn pudding. She would always make layers of corn pudding and stuff it with very well seasoned ground meat. Corn pudding is kind of like a creamy deconstructed corn bread, in case you never had it! I loved going to grandma's house and smelling the aroma of sweet corn being cooked. With this recipe I take a little shortcut using corn mix but the results are pretty similar. I always look at my mom as she's about to take her first bite, because I can see the warm memories of my grandma flooding back to her. My grandma was the sweetest angel, and to make something that brings the memory of her back is completely priceless.

MAKES 8 SERVINGS | *Prep time* 5 minutes | *Cook time* 45 minutes

WHAT YOU'LL NEED

- 8 oz corn muffin mix

- 1 can whole kernel corn, drained

- 1 can creamed corn, NOT drained

- 1 cup sour cream

- ½ cup salted melted butter

LET'S DO THIS!

Preheat the oven to 350°F.

In a bowl mix the ingredients together and pour into a greased 8 x 8 baking pan, cook and cover for 45 to 50 minutes, or until lightly brown. It's not called "Easy Peasy" for nothin'!

Heaven Sent Potato Salad

I remember the first barbecue that Rich and I hosted together. He was still living at his bachelor pad, and I was just coming to help him out to host his family. I really wanted to impress them, so I told Rich to put some meats on the grill and I would take care of all the side dishes. When he asked me what kind of side dishes I was making, I named a few that you will see in this book: pasta salad, spinach-based salad, and of course, potato salad. I guess potato salad was his favorite because I saw his eyes light up when I said it. At that time, we were at the beginning of our relationship and just getting to know each other. Home run for me!

I was still learning little things about him and now I knew potato salad was his favorite. Rich asked me what kind of potato salad I was making, and he started raving about his mom's potato salad (Rich always speaks so highly and full heartedly about his late mom). He's a tough guy but his voice cracks when he talks about her. He was just so curious about my preparation and asking me about all the ingredients I use and kept telling me how amazing his mom's was. Her potatoes were perfectly cooked, she added little bacon bits, she used hard boiled eggs, and even though he does not like them, they were a match made in heaven for that recipe. He mentioned that it was a mayo-based salad and there was one more ingredient he couldn't put his finger on, but it was what made it so tasty.

At that point I had his really high expectations, and I was even nervous to start cutting my potatoes. I used all the same ingredients that Rich said his mom used but I was eager to still make it my own. So, I added mustard to the mayo base. When the time came to present the salad to everyone, Rich took a bite, looked at me and said, "This tastes just like my mom's, thank you!" and then gave me a kiss. He couldn't stop talking about how good it was and later he asked me what ingredients I used. I named them all and when I told him I added mustard he said, "That's it, that's the key ingredient!" It literally brought tears to my eyes and melted my heart to be able to recreate his mother's potato salad. And I have no doubt, his mother sent me that special ingredient straight from heaven.

MAKES 8 SERVINGS   *Prep time* 20 minutes | *Cook time* 15 minutes

WHAT YOU'LL NEED

- 2 lbs red potatoes, peeled and diced
- 4 eggs, diced
- ¼ cup bacon, cooked and chopped)
- ½ cup green onions, chopped

- ½ cup mayonnaise
- ½ cup sour cream
- 2 tbsp white wine vinegar
- 1 tsp Dijon mustard
- salt and pepper to taste

LET'S DO THIS!

Wash the potatoes, peel them, and dice them into bite size pieces, about an inch or inch and a half. Put them in a pot and cover them with just enough water and cook them until tender. Make sure you don't overcook the potatoes. The cooking time will depend on the size of the potato chunks. Check them with a fork because they should be soft but not be mushy!

When the potatoes are done, drain the water and set aside to cool off.

In a separate pot, boil some water and once the water is at a good boil, delicately submerge the eggs. An egg should take about 7 minutes to cook. Remove the eggs, peel them, and slice them into smaller pieces.

Cook the bacon and chop it once it is finished.

To make the dressing mixture, mix the mayo, sour cream, white wine vinegar, and the mustard. Add one tablespoon of milk if the dressing needs to be loosened up.

Mix everything with the potatoes, eggs, bacon, and green onion and refrigerate until cool and it will be ready to be served. You will taste this and see why it is truly heaven sent!

Mexican Street Corn

Every time I go back home to Peru, my dad always makes sure he takes me to as many restaurants as he can. If it was up to him, he would make fancy breakfast, lunch, and dinner reservations every single day. But instead, I always ask him to take me to the little holes in the wall rather than those fancy places. The food is always made with so much love in a hole in the wall, and I am pretty simple. I always search for authentic flavors and real stories. Every time I travel to Mexico it is no different. I like to have street tacos, agua frescas, and of course street corn. Going through the streets outside Playa del Carmen has created some of my best food memories, and every time I make Mexican Street Corn at home, it brings me back there.

MAKES 4 SERVINGS | *Prep time* 5 minutes | *Cook time* 12-15 minutes

WHAT YOU'LL NEED

- 4 ears corn
- ¼ cup crema agria (sour cream will work just as well)
- ¼ cup mayonnaise
- ½ cup Mexican cotija cheese, crumbled
- ¼ tsp salt
- juice and zest 1 lime
- ¼ cup cilantro, finely chopped
- ½ tsp chipotle chili powder

LET'S DO THIS!

Heat the grill to roughly 400°F. You can grill the corn with the husk on or off. (I prefer the husk off, so I get nice grill marks on the corn, and it gives it a nice grilled favor).

If you choose to leave the husk on, let the corn soak in water for about 10 minutes before grilling. If you choose the husk off, lightly spray each cob with cooking spray.

Place the corn on the grill for roughly 12 to 15 minutes, turning the cobs a quarter turn every 3 to 4 minutes.

Mix the ingredients to make all the sauce: sour cream, mayonnaise, lime juice, and zest the salt and fresh cilantro.

When the corn comes off the grill, generously top each cob with the sauce. Top it off with the crumbled cotija cheese and chili powder. You will love it!

Classic (Not Rocket Science) Roasted Rosemary Potatoes

Cooking isn't rocket science (even though sometimes I like to act like a mad scientist in the kitchen). I have times where I feel like I've invented something totally unique with my recipes and other times I just like to stick to a more traditional classic that I know everybody loves. These rosemary potatoes are a simple and staple dish in my house. I try to cook them perfectly, nice and crispy on the outside, tender on the inside and filled with flavorful spices. These potatoes go great with any condiment of choice, or they can be delicious just on their own. Enjoy!

MAKES 6 SERVINGS *Prep time* 10 minutes | *Cook time* 1 hour

WHAT YOU'LL NEED

- 2 lbs baby potatoes (if small, cut in half or quarter if too large)
- 2 tbsp olive oil
- 4 garlic cloves, minced
- 2 tbsp freshly chopped rosemary
- kosher salt to taste
- freshly ground black pepper to taste

LET'S DO THIS!

Preheat the oven to 400°F.

In a bowl, add the cut potatoes, olive oil, garlic, rosemary, and season generously with salt and pepper.

Mix everything up and place on a sheet pan. Place in the oven and roast until crispy stirring occasionally for about 1 hour to 1 hour 15 minutes.

Remove from the oven and serve. So simple and so delicious!

Brussels Sprouts with Cranberries

I don't think I can blame my children for not eating brussels sprouts for the longest time. If I was just going to cut them in half and give it to them boiled or simply roasted there is really nothing fun to look forward to. I get it! But, for me, every time I eat brussels sprouts it reminds me of my grandmother. She would love them made in a very simple way, roasted with salt, pepper, and a little bit of lemon. I would always try to get out of eating them no matter what. So, when I had kids, I decided to change my brussels sprout game and take them up a notch. Now I roast them, and I add cranberries, honey, and walnuts. When these come out of the oven they do not last more than five minutes! They go great with any dish, but I myself like them with roasted chicken, and you definitely need to try them with any big holiday meal.

MAKES 6 SERVINGS **Prep time** 10 minutes | **Cook time** 25 minutes

WHAT YOU'LL NEED

- 1 ½ lbs Brussels sprouts, stemf and cut in half lengthwise
- 3 tbsp extra virgin olive oil
- ½ cup dried cranberries (previously soaked in warm water so they can plump up)
- ½ cup pecans, roughly chopped
- 2 tbsp honey
- salt and pepper to taste

LET'S DO THIS!

Preheat the oven to 425°F.

Line a baking sheet with parchment paper.

To prepare your Brussels sprouts, trim the nubby ends, and remove any discolored or damaged leaves, cut each sprout in half lengthwise from the flat base to the top!

In a bowl, mix the Brussels sprouts with the olive oil, salt and pepper, and toss them well.

Arrange all the Brussels sprouts evenly flat side down on the lined baking sheet, then roast the sprouts for about 20 minutes. Halfway through roasting make sure to toss the sprouts so they are all evenly roasted!

When they are almost done, remove them from the oven. Add the pecans and cranberries, then drizzle them with honey and pop back in the oven for an extra five minutes. Ooh, I love the smell!

Remove from the oven, mix them all well and serve.

Those Tiny Hands

I used to be the mom who was always worried I'd end up with modeling clay in the carpet and paint on the walls. Sophia and Gianna, being my older girls, didn't get to enjoy many of those messy moments. There is almost a ten year age difference between my middle child Gianna and my baby Alexandria. In those ten years I matured, I grew as a person, and I went through something that changed my life. I miscarried on my second trimester, and it was completely devastating. Never in a million years I would have thought that would happen to me since I had a history of healthy and easy pregnancies. I was truly in shock, and I really did experience the pain of loss.

After I healed from my miscarriage, I was blessed with another pregnancy and a beautiful child. Alexandria is so full of life: she is creative, has a spunky personality that can light up any room, and she has a contagious laugh, but she also has a wild side. While Sophia and Gianna were angels when they were little, God was preparing me for what was about to come. I was going to need to have patience, be more understanding, embrace the mess, and nurture that curiosity and zest for life that Alex has. Carpets can be vacuumed, walls can be repainted, and clothes can be cleaned, but building those memories and allowing a child to express themselves and grow their own personality is something you can't put a price on. Who cares if the cookies have an extra cup of sugar? Those cookies will be the "sweetest" cookies you've ever had in your life! If they choose to lick the spatula, they will learn what double dipping is, and if they eat the raw batter just make sure you have antacid handy in the cabinet. 😆 It was important to me to share with you these kid-friendly recipes so you could have those tiny hands in the kitchen. They grow up so much faster than you think and in a blink of an eye!

So, trust me, take those tiny hands into the kitchen with you and let's all have some fun!

Garlic Toast Pizzettes

I remember back in Peru when I was little going to the supermarket with my dad, my mom, and brother. Usually those were the nights when my dad wanted to choose all the meats and special cheeses and get everything to make homemade pizzas. My mom would make the dough and my dad would finish the pizzas. My brother and I would get involved as well and we always made it such a fun night. The memories of my parents having wine and cocktails in the kitchen and getting flour all over our faces and clothes are memories I will cherish forever. My brother and I would anxiously wait to see our creations coming out of the oven. Being little, there was a huge sense of accomplishment and satisfaction being able to eat what we just made. I love the idea of family pizza, but it can take a lot of time! So, I make these Garlic Toast Pizzettes now in a much easier way than the one I grew up with. But the one thing that stays the same is having my girls help and bringing the family closer together. If you want to try cooking and getting your littles involved, this is a fabulous dish and is a great opportunity to get a little messy.

MAKES 8 SERVINGS   *Prep time* 5 minutes | *Cook time* 10 minutes

WHAT YOU'LL NEED

- 8 slices Texas garlic toast bread

- 1 cup pizza sauce

- 1 ½ cups shredded mozzarella cheese

- 25 to 30 pepperoni slices (you can substitute the pepperoni with ham, cooked sausage, any vegetable pizza topping, or simply leave this plain)

LET'S DO THIS!

Preheat the oven to 425°F.

Place the garlic bread on a baking sheet, and spread about 2 to 3 tablespoons of pizza sauce on each piece of garlic bread.

Top with the shredded cheese and pepperoni (or topping of choice).

Place in the oven for eight to ten minutes, or until the cheese is nice and melted and the bottom is golden brown.

Remove from oven. Serve and enjoy!

Double Trouble Strawberries

Chocolate covered strawberries are something that I've been doing with my girls since they were very little. Half of the chocolate would actually make it onto the strawberries and the other half would end up in their mouth and all over their cute little faces from literally licking the spatula. For this version I have added a little surprise. Shhh! Don't tell anyone! You hollow out the strawberry and fill it with caramel and it makes it extra sweet. They are a tasty treat, that gives the kiddos a chance to get a messy face in the kitchen!

MAKES 18 SERVINGS   *Prep time* 15 minutes

WHAT YOU'LL NEED

- 18 strawberries hulled
- 1 cup Oak Hill Farms caramel your choice
- 2 cups semi-sweet chocolate chips, melted
- 1 tbsp coconut oil

LET'S DO THIS!

Make sure the strawberries are washed and dried. Cut the stem off of the strawberry so they are able to be hulled.

Cut the bottom tip off of the strawberry so they can actually stand upright.

Fill them with the Oak Hill Farms caramel of your choice, then put them in the fridge for 5 to 10 minutes to allow the caramel to firm up.

In the meantime, melt your chocolate chips in the microwave with one tablespoon of coconut oil. The coconut oil allows the chocolate to become loose and smooth, this makes it easier for dipping! Check this mixture every thirty seconds, stirring until they are fully melted.

Take the strawberries out of the fridge and dip them into the chocolate mixture covering them completely.

Place them on a piece of parchment paper standing up, this prevents the caramel from dripping out.

Carla's Tip!

You can dress the chocolate covered strawberries up with sprinkles, shredded coconut, chocolate designs, or just serve them plain as they are! They are so sweet and delicious!

Best Ever Burger Sliders

This recipe is a winner in my house! And it is so simple with the Hawaiian rolls I use. You can have the same concept and make different variations. Either way it's always going to be a win-win for everybody. I love to cook but I really don't like to grill, so the idea of a burger slider without having to grill is my idea of a perfect happy medium. And they are so versatile! You can change the cheeses, you can add extra toppings, but regardless of how you want to get creative with them, they are always going to be a hit! Get ready to make double batches because people are going to be having several, I guarantee you.

MAKES 12 SLIDERS   *Prep time* Less than 15 minutesv

WHAT YOU'LL NEED

- 1 lb ground beef

- ½ tbsp oil

- 1 tsp salt

- 1 tsp black pepper

- 1 tsp garlic powder

- 1 medium yellow onion, finely diced

- 12 slices cheddar cheese

- 1 pack 12 Hawaiian rolls

- 1 tbsp melted butter

LET'S DO THIS!

Preheat the oven to 350°F.

In a large skillet, over medium/high heat add the oil, diced onions, and the ground beef. Break the ground beef with a spatula while cooking. Season with salt, black pepper, and garlic powder.

Sauté over medium heat until the ground beef is cooked through.

Cut the Hawaiian rolls in half. Don't cut them individually leave all the bottoms and tops together but cut the entire layer of the bottoms away from the tops. Place the bottom half of the roll on a baking sheet lined with parchment paper or aluminum foil.

Spread 6 slices of cheese covering the bottom of the bun. Add the ground beef mixture spreading evenly over the cheese, then top it off with the remaining 6 slices of cheese and add the tops of the buns.

Brush the bun tops with the melted butter. Place the baking sheet in the oven and bake off for 10 to 12 minutes at 350°F until the cheese is melted and the tops of the bun are golden brown!

Blow Your Mind Microwave Brownies

These brownies take me back in time to when I was ten years old. They remind me of the fun memories I had growing up. My neighborhood girlfriends and I would split up into pairs and make teams to compete against each other in a dessert cook off - a competition created by yours truly (of course!). I don't even think Top Chef was a thing back then! We would get our brothers and guy friends to be the judges. Once they tried all the desserts, they would cast their votes and the winners would get the bragging rights for being the best baker. This recipe seemed to always be the favorite. I always wanted to change it up, but my mom would never let me use the stove or oven when I was unsupervised. So, I always had to think outside the box and make desserts with what I was allowed to use, and that was the microwave. I was probably eight years old when I was first introduced to a microwave, and I remember they came with these little booklets of easy recipes. That is where this recipe comes from: my first microwave. It is a great recipe to share with your children and let them be creative in the kitchen. BONUS! You can even let them do it entirely on their own because there is no stovetop or oven needed. I usually just top it off with powdered sugar, but if my sweet tooth needs an extra boost, I will add a coat of hot fudge or caramel.

MAKES 6-8 SERVINGS   *Prep time* Less than 5 minutes | *Cook time* 4-6 minutes

WHAT YOU'LL NEED

- 1 stick unsalted butter, melted

- 2 eggs

- 1 cup granulated sugar

- 1 tsp pure vanilla extract

- ¾ cup flour

- ¼ cup cocoa powder

- 1 tsp baking powder

- Optional Garnishes: powdered sugar, Oak Hill Farms Caramel, or Oak Hill Farms Hot Fudge

LET'S DO THIS!

In a bowl add the melted butter, the two eggs, the cup of sugar, and the pure vanilla extract. Mix very well.

Add the flour, the cocoa powder, and the baking powder—mixing all ingredients together well.

Pour the mixture into an 8 x 8 microwaveable dish (Pyrex works great).

Insert the dish into the microwave for 4 to 6 minutes on high. This should not take longer than six minutes, it will depend on the power of the microwave you have. Once the brownie is no longer jiggly in the middle it will be ready!

Layer with powdered sugar, Oak Hill Farms Caramel or Oak Hill Farms Hot Fudge, and serve.

Serve while still nice and hot!

Picky Eater Approved Taco Sticks

Alexandria, my youngest, is a really picky eater, but I find that if I give her food in a fun way, she actually enjoys eating it. I have done everything from buying molds to cutting her fruit and sandwiches in fun shapes using cookie cutters to making her dishes colorful and cute. But at the end of the day, the quality of food is what counts too, right? These taco sticks are a really easy snack or if you make several, they can be a good dinner for the picky eater in your house! And believe me, it doesn't only satisfy the picky eater. Everybody in your house will have their hands on these. They are just easy, tasty, and most importantly fun!

MAKES 10 TACO STICKS | *Prep time* 10 minutes | *Cook time* 12 minutes

WHAT YOU'LL NEED

- 1 lb ground beef

- 1 packet taco seasoning mix

- 1 tube pizza dough

- 5 colby jack cheese sticks, halved

- 4 tbsp melted butter

- 1 tsp garlic powder

- 1 tsp dried parsley

LET'S DO THIS!

Preheat the oven to 450°F.

Lightly coat a baking sheet with non-stick spray and set aside.

In a skillet, cook the ground beef, breaking apart with a wooden spoon or spatula until fully brown and crumbled.

Drain any fat and season with the packet of taco seasoning. Stir until fully coated, then remove from the heat and let it cool to room temperature!

Spread the pizza dough out until it is flat, cut in half lengthwise, then make 4 cuts up and down creating a total of 10 small rectangles.

Place about a tablespoon or more of the taco beef in the center of each piece of pizza dough. Top with a half piece of the cheese stick. Roll the dough up, making sure to pinch all the seams closed.

In a bowl combine the melted butter with the garlic powder and parsley. Brush this mixture on top of the cheesy taco sticks.

Bake for 10 to 12 minutes or until golden brown on top.

Serve hot with your favorite taco toppings.

Is It Happy Hour Yet?

For real . . . is it? This is a judgment-free zone, guys. I won't mind if you get your drink on early as long as you don't mind me having a mimosa for breakfast. ☺

All joking aside, there is just something great about hanging out with friends, entertaining guests, or relaxing after a long day at work with a nice refreshing cocktail. If you're like me, you get tired of always sipping on the same old thing, so I always try to find a way to spice things up. Our hot honey cocktails are some of my favorites because it gives your "tipsy" a kick. You will find a few of those and many other cocktails in this section. I highly recommend you try them all!

Just do me a favor and drink responsibly.
In Carla's world, that means don't leave a drop,
and have a taxi driver on speed dial!

Bee Fiery

Have you ever heard of a bee sting cocktail? It is one of the best gin cocktail recipes and it is made with honey and jalapeño. I heard about it from my husband, Rich, who is really an old country soul who listens to Kenny Rogers and loves gin! I am not a big gin drinker but when we finished our first batch of hot honey, I wanted to try something different with gin. (In case you're wondering, hot honey is my husband's secret blend of spices with our wildflower honey, so I can't share all the secrets.) I didn't want to do the common bee sting, so I went back to my fiery Latin roots and came up with this Bee Fiery cocktail. It gets our hot honey in it instead of jalapeño, but I also add some refreshing grapefruit juice and fresh basil. So, if you're feeling feisty, try Bee Fiery!

MAKES 1 COCKTAIL

Prep time Less than 5 minutes | *Mixing time* Less than 5 minutes

WHAT YOU'LL NEED

- 2 oz gin

- 2 oz grapefruit juice

- 1 tbsp Oak Hill Farms Hot Honey

- juice half a lime

- ice

- Optional Garnishes: lime wedge and basil leaves

LET'S DO THIS!

In a shaker add the gin, grapefruit juice, lime juice, and a tablespoon of hot honey. Mix well and add the ice. Close and shake very well! Shake it, girl!

Strain the mixture into a glass with ice.

Garnish with a lime wedge and a few basil leaves and serve.

Raspberry 'n Lemon Bubbly

I think there is something so pretty about carrying a glass of champagne while having brunch. And I love pretty things and getting together with friends, so I always look for an excuse to have a tea party or brunch with my girlfriends at least once a year. I just love to feel super girly and wear a pretty dress, have nice hors d'oeuvres, little finger foods, and of course champagne. If you don't have champagne, Prosecco will do. Even though I don't love carbonated drinks, I love a good Raspberry 'n Lemon Bubbly! It's super easy to make, refreshing and goes great at any Sunday brunch.

MAKES 1 COCKTAIL   *Prep time* *Less than 5 minutes*

WHAT YOU'LL NEED

- 1 scoop lemon sorbet

- 1 scoop raspberry sorbet

- 6 oz Prosecco

- fresh raspberries

- lemon wheels

LET'S DO THIS!

Add 1 scoop of each of the lemon and raspberry sorbet into a glass.

Add the Prosecco and serve immediately.

Garnish with fresh raspberries and a lemon wedge.

Carla's Tip!

You can make this into a Frozen Raspberry 'n Lemon Bubbly if you add a little bit of ice and put it into a blender. I always recommend wearing a wide brimmed hat while sipping on this, too. Raspberry 'n Lemon Bubbly gives you instant Queen Status!

Straight from Peru Pisco Sour

Pisco Sour is a traditional Peruvian cocktail that has become famous around the world as more and more Peruvians try to create awareness of our traditions and our food in the last 10 to 15 years. I am lucky to say that my mom's side of the family owns vineyards where they produce pisco (an authentic Peruvian brandy). I will say this though—do not take pisco sours lightly, you may not feel anything after the first or the second one but by the third it can knock you down and lay you out!

I have a funny story with me and pisco sours. When I left Peru to come to America, I was still very young, so I hadn't had the chance to drink very much of anything and didn't get to enjoy many of these delicious cocktails. I've been going back home many times to visit since I left, but let me remind you, I've lived in the states longer than I lived in Peru, so I feel like I am completely half and half! I went back to Peru about three years ago and went out with all my girlfriends from high school. They wanted to celebrate that I was visiting, and it was like a big reunion for us all. Many of us live in different countries around the world now so it was a great way to come together and have some good girl fun.

Well, one of my girlfriends is a phenomenal singer and it just so happened she was singing that night, so we went to support her and spend some time together. We started the tab with a pisco sour for each of us—then we decided to add another round and another and another. There were seven of us and we each ordered a round, so we had seven pisco sours each and let me tell you, I woke up with the worst hangover the next day. And not only was I hungover, but I had a dental appointment that morning! Oh boy. It's a very good thing that one of my friends who happened to be at the party is also my dentist. She was pretty much in the same shape that I was in, so we were both very understanding when an hour-long dental appointment took five hours because of all the bathroom runs. Even though this memory had a rough after-effect, it still didn't make me change my mind on pisco sours. They are still one of my favorite drinks but here is my warning to you: stop at one or two and don't have SEVEN like I did!

MAKES 1 COCKTAIL *Prep time* Less than 5 minutes

WHAT YOU'LL NEED

- 3 oz Pisco
- 1 oz fresh squeezed lime juice
- 1 oz simple syrup
- 1 fresh egg white
- 1 dash bitters

LET'S DO THIS!

Combine the Pisco, lime, simple syrup, and the egg in a shaker without ice. Shake vigorously until the egg white is foamy, about 10 seconds.

Add ice to the shaker and shake again very hard until well chilled, about another 10 seconds.

Strain into a cocktail glass, dash bitters on top of the egg white foam.

Carla's Tips!

1. If you want to make more than one cocktail you can multiply the ingredients by the number of glasses and put everything in the blender, that is the easiest way to make a bigger batch and have everything ready at the same time. Pisco is perfect for a party!

2. To make the simple syrup, combine 1 cup of water and 1 cup of granulated sugar in a small saucepan, bring it to a quick boil letting the sugar dissolve, and then let it cool completely.

3. You can keep in the fridge and use as needed.

Refreshing Tropical Sangria

There is nothing better for a hot summer get-together than a big glass of Refreshing Tropical Sangria! Traditionally, sangria is made with a peach base or brandy, but you should know me by now, I can't follow the rules. I took sangria on a vacation to the tropics and added a surprising juice to the mix. So, if you are a lover of tropical flavors and most importantly wine, then this will not let you down. It is crisp and refreshing and because you can make it in a big batch you won't have to worry about serving your guest cocktails all night. So, that means you can get your drink on and break out your best salsa moves!

MAKES 4-6 SERVINGS   *Prep time* 10 minutes

WHAT YOU'LL NEED

- 1 bottle white wine (I prefer to use a Pinot Grigio or Sauvignon Blanc)

- 4 oz brandy

- 2 oz Triple Sec

- 1 cup orange juice

- 1 cup pineapple juice

- 2 oz simple syrup (equal parts water and sugar brought to a boil for 2 minutes in a small saucepan and cooled)

- ½ cup apricot juice or peach juice (if you don't find apricot or peach juice you can make your own by peeling the peaches frozen or fresh. Remove the pits and blend with a little bit water)

- Garnishes: fresh peaches, oranges, pineapple, and apple slices (you can use all these fruits or whatever is your favorite)

LET'S DO THIS!

Place all ingredients in a pitcher, stir to mix well.

Refrigerate for at least 2 hours and up to 48 (the longer the better).

Serve over Ice. Does it get any easier?

Screaming Margarita

Okay, okay, the name of this drink might sound weird, but don't be afraid! This margarita will definitely make you scream, but it will be cheers of happiness! The first time I ever had a drink that had any heat, it was a jalapeno inspired margarita. After the first sip I thought it was phenomenal, and that the heat in the alcohol was simply genius. Once we started producing our hot honey at the farm, I thought it would be a great idea to use it for making cocktails. It has the sweetness that a cocktail needs, but it adds the heat for that tasty surprise. The Screaming Margarita is probably my favorite cocktail. I make with the hot honey, and it definitely will not disappoint. They say money can't buy happiness, but it can buy tequila and that is pretty much the same thing!

MAKES 1 COCKTAIL

Prep time Less than 5 minutes | *Mixing time* Less than 5 minute

WHAT YOU'LL NEED

- 2 oz white tequila

- 1 oz lime juice

- 1 oz simple syrup (equal parts water and sugar brought to a boil for 2 minutes in a small saucepan and cooled)

- 1 tbsp hot honey

- lime wedge

- salt for the rim

LET'S DO THIS!

In a shaker mix the tequila, lime juice, hot honey, simple syrup, add ice; close and shake very well.

Salt the rim of a margarita glass, add ice, and strain the mixture into it.

Garnish with a lime wedge and serve.

Strawberry Mint Smash

This cocktail reminds me of a mojito but with the sweetness of strawberries. I love to add fresh mint to many of my cocktails during summertime because it makes them so refreshing and fragrant! This one does the trick! It is delicious, light, boozy, and a big crowd pleaser if you are choosing to entertain guests. So, just when you think those hot summer days can't get any brighter, just add a delicious, fresh Strawberry Mint Smash, and make sure to put your shades on, kick back, and relax!

MAKES 1 DRINK   *Prep time* Less than 5 minutes

WHAT YOU'LL NEED

- 5 ripe strawberries, stems off and cut in half
- 1 tbsp Oak Hill Farms Honey
- 5 to 7 fresh mint leaves
- 2 oz vodka
- 1 oz lime juice
- seltzer or club soda
- ice
- Optional Garnishes: lime wedges, strawberries, and fresh mint

LET'S DO THIS!

Put the halved strawberries, mint leaves, and honey in the bottom of a cocktail shaker and muddle well with the bottom of a wooden spoon or muddler.

Add the lime juice, vodka, and ice. Close the shaker and shake very well.

In a glass, rub a piece of lime along the rim and dip it in sugar, add ice cubes to the glass.

Strain the shaker mixture into the glass and top it off with club soda or seltzer. Garnish with the fresh mint, strawberries, and a lime wedge.

Cheers!

Save the Best for Last

There is not a complete meal without dessert and no celebration without cake, right? Every meal, I try to pace myself and leave space for dessert. I don't know about you, but I love to save the best for last because it gives me extra satisfaction. I attribute this feeling to my daddy, and I'll tell you why . . .

When I graduated high school and it was time to go off to college, I told my dad that I wanted to become an attorney just like him. I'm the only daughter and I wanted to make my daddy proud. My dad comes from a family very focused on education, so lawyers and doctors were the common profession for them. I started going to school to pursue a career in law, but I had zero interest. I was skipping class and going to pool parties until my dad found out. He sat me down and had a serious conversation with me. I had an ultimatum: to find out what I wanted to do with my life. I thought about it and realized that what I enjoyed the most was cooking. Let's remember that being a chef back in the day wasn't the cool trend it is today. It was not common, and far from conservative, so when I had to meet my dad to talk about my future, I told him (shaking inside) that I wanted to be a pastry chef. He looked at me, smiled and said: why don't you go to culinary school and get a diploma in culinary arts first? And if you really want to specialize in pastry, you can go back and study that. Save the best for last my dear. And that's what I did. I finished culinary school and then I went back to do pastry, so I pretty much ended my studies with the icing on the cake (no pun intended)! I enjoyed every day of school, never skipped a class, and baking became my way to release stress and be truly happy. When I wake up every day excited to do what I love most, I think of my daddy's unconditional love and support, his words of wisdom, and his requests to always make a double batch of dessert!

I hope you enjoy all these recipes because I saved my best for last! ☺

Alfajores

This is my most precious recipe, my biggest secret, and quite possibly the Holy Grail of this book!

Alfajores are a Peruvian staple. They are a shortbread-type cookie sandwich filled with dulce de leche that melts in your mouth. It is a recipe that people have raved about every time I make it. I have never shared this recipe because I always wanted to keep it as a family secret and pass it on down to my girls. I used to have tons of recipes like that, and as I grew up and got more mature, I realized: why would I keep them only for me? If my recipes bring such joy to the ones I make them for, shouldn't they be shared?

My oldest daughter Sophia is the only other person in my house who knows how to make Alfajores. When I told her I was going to add this recipe in the book, at first she didn't want me to do it. We actually almost had a fight over it. I explained to her the great thing about being able to write this book, is that now we can share some of our amazing recipes with the world and everyone can now get to enjoy them. It took a little bit of time for her to process it but in the end, she agreed. And really aren't those the types of moments and lessons that we want to be able to share with our children? These are the lessons where they can learn to grow and understand that being selfish is never the right answer. I am so proud of my baby for being able to understand the value of giving something that is so special to her to others.

So, with Sophia's permission, we are sharing our Alfajores with you. She has truly mastered this recipe, and her only advice is to not be like mommy and walk away from the kitchen while the cookies are in the oven. You need to stick around and make sure you check them so they don't burn on the bottom. Believe me I have lost my patience, walked away, and burned several batches in my life. So, without further ado—here is the wow factor, the headliner, the showstopper of this book. I can't wait for you to try them!

MAKES 40 SMALL COOKIES

Prep time 30-45 minutes | *Cook time* 15-18 minutes

WHAT YOU'LL NEED

- 1 cup all-purpose flour

- 1 cup corn starch

- 1 cup unsalted butter, at room temperature (equivalent to 2 sticks butter)

- 6 tbsp powdered sugar

- 2 cans dulce de leche
  (I use the "La Lechera brand" because it is thick enough and is the perfect consistency for this cookie, you can find it on the ethnic aisle)

- Additional Tools:
  Cookie cutter. I use a one-inch scalloped round cookie cutter. (You can use whatever shape you prefer.)

LET'S DO THIS!

Preheat the oven to 350°F.

In a large bowl mix all the ingredients: flour, corn starch, butter, and powdered sugar. Make sure you work the dough well. Let it rest in the fridge for about 30 minutes.

Remove from the fridge. On top of a floured surface in your kitchen, roll the dough into a disk getting it to about ¼ inch thick. Using a cookie cutter, cut the cookies and place them on a non-stick baking sheet, about 1 inch apart.

Cook them for about 15 to 18 minutes, until they start turning golden but make sure to check the bottom of the cookie while they are cooking because sometimes, they tend to brown really fast.

After the cookies are done, remove from the oven. Create mini cookie sandwiches by filling the cookie with some of the dulce de leche and adding another cookie on top.

Sprinkle with a generous amount of powdered sugar.

These cookies will keep for several days in an airtight container.

Cheesecake Churro Bars

I know, your mouth is watering already just from the name. This is a newer recipe for me. I saw the idea of mixing cheesecake and churros online and I decided to give it a whirl myself because it was too easy not to. I remember the day that I made it I was in a rush because I was actually traveling to Vermont for work, and I needed to get to the airport. Before I left, I wanted to make something tasty to showcase on my Instagram account (the struggle of creating content).

I couldn't believe how quick they really were to make. When I took them out of the oven, I was already running late so I didn't even have the chance to try them. I asked my mom to please cut them up for me and take a few pictures so I could share them. She brought them to the girls who were working at our farm on that day to put them to the taste test. I had barely made it passed the security at the airport when my phone started lighting up. I was getting all these messages telling me they were to die for, where did I get the idea, can I please have the recipe … Everyone who tried one was just raving about them. Of course, when I got home two days later there wasn't one crumb leftover, so I had to make another batch just to try them out for myself, and let me tell you they were right, these things are delicious! The reason I added it to this book is not only because they are so tasty but because it is a very simple one, two, three type of recipe that you will absolutely love, and can make over and over forever.

MAKES 18 SQUARES *(depending on the size they are cut)*

Prep time 15 minutes | *Cook time* 25-30 minutes

WHAT YOU'LL NEED

Bars

- 2 (8 oz) tubes refrigerated crescent rolls
- 2 (8 oz) packages cream cheese, softened
- 1 cup granulated sugar
- 1 tsp pure vanilla extract

Topping

- ½ cup granulated sugar
- 1 tbsp ground cinnamon
- ½ cup unsalted butter, melted

LET'S DO THIS!

Preheat the oven to 350°F. Spray a 9 x 13 baking dish with cooking spray. Unroll one of the tubes of crescent rolls and spread the dough in a single layer on the bottom of the prepared baking dish, making sure all the dough is pressed and sealed together.

In a mixer, beat together the cream cheese with the sugar until nice and fluffy in texture, then add the pure vanilla extract and beat again until well incorporated.

Gently spread this cream cheese mixture over the top layer of the crescent dough and make sure it is nice and even.

Unroll the other tube of the crescent roll dough and lay it over the top of the cream cheese mixture in a single layer, making sure that you are pressing all the precut triangles together to seal them so it looks like one big piece of dough!

On the side, in a small bowl mix together the half cup of granulated sugar and the tablespoon of cinnamon, and mix together until combined and set aside.

Melt the butter and pour it evenly on top of the crescent roll layered dish. Sprinkle the cinnamon sugar mixture over the top of the melted butter in an even layer. It will look like it is a lot but trust me it will be just perfect.

Bake for 25 to 30 minutes until the top is nice brown and crunchy and the center of the dish is set. Oh, your kitchen will smell so good! Let it cool slightly and if you like you can refrigerate it and cut it into pieces (I prefer it warm though!).

Brioche Bread Pudding

Every time I think about bread pudding, I think of my dad. He would go into the kitchen after my mom would make bread pudding and grab a spoon to take a little sliver of the pudding! Then he would leave the spoon in the pan and walk away. He would pass back by again and take another little sliver and another, and that's how he would finish the entire pan in just a few hours. Bread pudding is something that we always had at home because my mom never wasted anything! She would put that stale bread to good use, and she made bread pudding with it quite often. She would add some raisins, and she would make a brown sugar syrup that went on top. The version I make is a little different. Sometimes I use stale bread but most of the time when I make bread pudding, I make it as a dessert to show off a little, so I will make it with fresh bread. I usually use Brioche or Challah bread, and I make a whiskey style sauce to go with it because it automatically reminds me of my dad (his favorite drink has always been whiskey on the rocks). When my dad comes to visit, I always make Brioche Bread Pudding, and he still does the same slivering trick in my house too.

Prep time 20 minutes | *Cook time* 1 hour

WHAT YOU'LL NEED

- 2 loaves Brioche bread, cut into 1-inch cubes
- 2 ½ cups heavy cream
- 1 ½ cups milk
- 3 large eggs
- 2 cups granulated sugar
- 2 tbsp pure vanilla extract
- 3 tbsp soft butter
- pinch salt
- Optional: 1 cup raisins, 4 tbsp whiskey

Sauce

- 1 stick unsalted butter (½ cup)
- 1 cup granulated sugar
- 1 large egg
- ½ cup whiskey

LET'S DO THIS!

Place the cup of raisins in a small bowl and cover with the whiskey so they can plump up, about 15 minutes.

Preheat the oven to 350°F.

Use the softened butter to cover the bottom and sides of a 9 x 13 glass or ceramic baking dish.

Place the cubed bread in a large mixing bowl and pour the heavy cream and milk over the bread. Mix the bread, milk, and cream with your hands until no large pieces of bread remain and the milk and the cream have been absorbed.

In a separate bowl, beat the eggs, add the sugar, salt, and pure vanilla extract, and mix well. Pour this over the milk, cream, and bread mixture, then add the raisins and mix well.

Pour this mixture in the buttered baking dish and bake until the liquid sets and the top starts to brown on the edges, about 40 to 50 minutes.

Remove from the oven and allow to cool as you make the sauce. Or if you are making ahead of time, allow it to cool down to room temperature. You can refrigerate for up to two days if you cover with aluminum foil.

For the whiskey sauce—you can make the sauce while the bread pudding is cooking or while it cools. Maybe you might sneak a sip of the whiskey … Don't worry, I won't tell!

Melt the butter in a saucepan over low heat, whisk the sugar and beaten egg into the melted butter over low heat, then stir the mixture constantly until the sauce is thick enough to coat the back of a spoon. Remove from the heat, add the whiskey to taste, and serve over top of the bread pudding.

Cinco Leches (5 Milks)

My kids always joke around with me, and they tell me that I am an over achiever. Yes, they make fun of me for having a competitive side. It's a healthy competitive, but still competitive. When I told them I was going to make Cinco Leches which translates in Spanish to "five milks", they said in sarcastic way, "Of course, you will make Cinco Leches, Mommy, why would you only keep them at three?" (They were referring to the Tres Leches traditional dessert, which translates to three milks.)

The truth is this dessert whether Tres or Cinco Leches always goes back to the basics: a nice spongy cake soaked into a mixture of milk with a nice vanilla flavor. Milk-soaked cake is very traditional in the majority of Hispanic countries. Growing up I never really knew about it, but it has become more popular in Peru as time has passed and is influenced more by Central American cuisine. I actually learned about Tres Leches when I first came to the United States about twenty years ago, but when I went back to visit Peru people had started making it, and back home they also make Cinco Leches! Of course, the Peruvian in me has adopted that, the more the merrier right? So, Cinco Leches it is!

WHAT YOU'LL NEED

Cake

- 6 eggs
- 2 cups granulated sugar
- 2 tsp pure vanilla extract
- 2 cups all-purpose flour
- 3 tsp baking powder
- ½ cup fresh milk
  (room temperature)

Milk Mixture

- 2 cans condensed milk
- 2 cans evaporated milk
- 2 cups heavy cream
- 2 cups coconut milk
- ¼ cup rum
- Optional Garnishes: fresh fruit,
  whipped cream, and/or Dulce de
  Leche

LET'S DO THIS!

In a mixer beat the eggs with the sugar and vanilla for about 10 minutes.

In a separate bowl, mix the flour with the baking powder and start incorporating it into the egg mixture. To do this, bring the mixture to a lower speed and gradually add half of the flour mixture, half of the milk, let it mix a little bit and add the other half of the flour and the other half of the milk until all the ingredients are well combined but do not over mix.

Get a Pyrex or oven proof container ready and grease it with butter or non-stick spray. Add the mixture to the container and bake it off at 325°F for 40 minutes.

Remove from the oven and with a fork add little holes to the entire cake.,

In a separate bowl, mix all of the milks with the rum. Pour this mixture over the cake letting it penetrate through the holes. Refrigerate the cake for at least an hour or two. You can serve with fresh fruit on top, and add whipped cream or Dulce de Leche, or simply serve as it is! It's delicious!!

Crème Caramel

My grandma always took me everywhere with her. If she was going away for the weekend or visiting family members, heading to the beach, birthdays, reunions, anything she did, I was right there by her side. I was her first grandchild, and we just had a very special relationship that I will cherish forever. Maybe my brother and cousins won't like to hear this, but I was my grandmother's favorite. Yep, she would always hug me and whisper that in my ear. The story I'm about to share is one of the funniest ones with her.

We were going to a family member's house to celebrate their daughter's fourth birthday, and my Uncle Hernan (my mom's baby brother) was going to drive us there. He always had so much patience and put so much care into my grandmother, always making sure that she wouldn't miss a party, and had a safe ride. A true gent! My grandma is the one who taught me to never show up to a house empty handed, but this time we had too much in our hands. She was bringing her famous fruit cake and a Crème Caramel (her staple dessert she would make for everyone she knew that was having a birthday). My uncle was helping my grandmother into the car and while he is doing that, he set the Crème Caramel on top of the roof of the car while he placed the fruitcake on my grandma's lap, then he puts me in the back seat and starts driving. Yes, I said starts driving! The Crème Caramel was still on top of the car, and we get about half a block down and all of a sudden, he remembers, "Gosh where is the Crème Caramel?"

We turned around to look and you wouldn't even believe it! The Crème Caramel had flown right onto the road, and it landed like nothing had happened. It was standing straight up, never flipped or anything, (well maybe just lost some of the juice). We stopped the car and went running down the street to check and (this is the part nobody knows) we picked it up, blew the little bit of dirt off, and we brought it to that party. Nobody knew what that cake went through to get there, but there wasn't one slice left when it was time to go.

MAKES 12 SERVINGS   *Prep time* Less than 10 minutes | *Cook time* 1 hour

WHAT YOU'LL NEED

Caramel

- 2 cups granulated sugar
- 1 cup water

Creme

- 3 cans condensed milk
- 3 cans evaporated milk
- 1 ½ tsp pure vanilla extract
- 12 eggs

LET'S DO THIS!

Preheat the oven to 325°F.

To make the caramel, in a saucepan cook the sugar and water until it becomes nice and golden brown in color. When it hits this color, immediately remove the saucepan from the heat and swirl in the pan to make it caramel. When it is ready, pour it in your cake pan of choice—I usually use a high round ten-inch pan, ensuring you cover the entire base by moving the caramel around.

In a blender blend together the condensed milk, the evaporated milk, the vanilla, and the eggs.

Pour this custard over the caramel mold, but after you pour it make sure you let it stand for about ten minutes so all of the bubbles that can be created at the moment of blending disappear and if you still see bubbles on top remove that foam with a spoon. You don't want any bubbles in your caramel!

You will need to get a bigger dish and you are going to need to do a double boiler in the oven, so to do that place the pan in a larger baking dish and fill the larger dish about halfway with boiling water and put it into the oven to bake for forty-five to fifty minutes at 325°F.

Check the custard at around 40 minutes by jiggling slightly. If it ripples like water, it is not ready, you need it to jiggle like jelly. Insert a knife in the middle and it should come out mostly clean with just a few streaks, but no clumps!

Remove from the oven and allow it to cool at room temperature inside the water bath.

Put it in the fridge for at least 4 to 5 hours, overnight is even better.

When you are ready to serve, run the knife along the edges pressing against the edge of the pan to avoid cutting the custard, just to make sure that it comes loose. Place a plate with raised edges on top of the pan and flip, make sure you use a plate that is going to hold the juice that comes out from the caramel.

Key Lime Meringue

Key Lime Meringue is the name that I have given this dessert which is really the best of both worlds: the creamy and tart key lime pie combined with the meringue of the lemon pie. I grew up on Key Lime Meringue—in Peru this dessert is a staple! Let me tell you a story about when my mother was pregnant with my brother. I was seven years old, so I can remember clearly my mom's cravings for Key Lime Meringue. She had a slice of this pie every single day during her pregnancy, and luckily for us we had a great little dessert shop three blocks from our house, where they made the best one. Every single day my mom and I would walk down there so she could get her pie fix. I could see it in her face how much she loved every single spoonful as she ate it.

Now let's fast forward to when my brother was born. Can you guess what his favorite dessert to this day is? Yep! Key Lime Meringue! You maybe would have thought he got enough when he was growing in her belly. Guess not!

Do you believe in that? When they say that your kids will end up liking what you craved while you were pregnant? When I was pregnant with Sophia my craving was cereal and milk, and to this day she will take a bowl of that over dinner. With Gianna it was crushed ice, and she has literally chipped teeth from her obsession with chewing on ice cubes. With Alexandria, I drank ice water by the gallon, and believe me I don't drink a quarter cup a day regularly, and now that girl drinks like a fish. So, after seeing how much my girls love the things I craved while I was pregnant with each of them, I know how much my brother loves Key Lime Meringue. I make sure to have all the ingredients on hand ready to welcome him with his favorite dessert every time he arrives to visit. Believe me if you have any doubts about this pie, take one look at this photo and I guarantee it will make your mouth water! If you make it once you will love it for life, and if you eat it while pregnant get ready to make it often because your children will be craving it just as much as my brother.

WHAT YOU'LL NEED

Filling

- 1 graham cracker pie crust
- 2 cans condensed milk
- 1 cup fresh squeezed lime juice
- 8 egg yolks

Meringue

- 8 egg whites
- 2 ½ cups granulated sugar
- 1 tsp pure vanilla extract
- pinch salt
- ½ tsp lime zest

LET'S DO THIS!

Make the Filling

Preheat your oven at 350°F.

In a large bowl, mix all the ingredients very well, and pour into the graham cracker crust.

Cook in the oven for 10 minutes, remove from the oven, and let it cool for another 10 to 15 minutes.

Make the Meringue

Raise the temperature of the oven to 450°F.

In the bowl, of a mixer add the egg whites and granulated sugar. On the side, add about 1 to 2 inches of water to a pot. You are going to do what is called a bain marie (or double boiler) where you will be placing the mixing bowl into the pot of water. Bring the water to a boil and start whisking the ingredients. You do this so the ingredients don't have direct contact with the fire, and it is not as harsh. Whisk constantly until the egg white mixture becomes warm to touch, to test use your little finger, you don't want it to be hot but just warm. Once it becomes warm remove the mixing bowl from the double boiler.

When you remove it from the heat, add the pure vanilla extract and the salt and continue mixing in the actual mixer, until the egg whites become an actual meringue. The consistency will be nice and compact and really shiny.

When the meringue is finished, put it into a pastry bag with a star tip and start decorating your pie on top. This is so much fun!

Put the pie back in the oven for another 5 to 10 minutes until it starts becoming nice and golden brown, once it gets this way remove it from the oven and let it cool.

Mooning for Mango Tart

When I was young, I spent a lot of time baking with my grandma. She was a nurse but when she retired, she decided to start taking classes for cake decorating and making desserts just for fun. She even took me to some of the classes with her! I enjoyed that so much. I think that's where my love for culinary comes from, baking with my grandma and literally making the best memories of my life. When I think of her, I always remember her baking in the kitchen. We got along so well, and I was just like her shadow, always following her around. She even bought me all my little baking tools so I could make my own mini version of whatever she was whipping up. We had a lot in common and one of our loves was fruit. We would go to the market together and get fruit, but not just by the pound or kilos, by the cases!! She would get cases of strawberries, plums, and mangos—whatever fruit you name she would get a case of. She would come home and share them with other family members. Oh, she would make little bags of different fruit and anyone who came to visit she would send home with one of the bags. It was like a party favor just for visiting! Her generosity is something that I have always admired. I mean, if you needed them, she would give you the shoes off of her own feet (and I'm not exaggerating!).

On one occasion when we came back from the market, and she started to split the fruit to share, when she got to the mango case, she asked, "Carlita, would you like a mango?" (She knew that it was my favorite fruit.) We started eating them at the table. Because they were so juicy, she gave me a tea towel to tuck inside my shirt and she did the same. So, there we were with tea towels in our shirts eating mango after mango. One mango, two mangos, three mangos and we were not stopping. They were so juicy that the juice was dripping down our chin, down our arms and while she is chewing, she gives me a wink and tells me we should finish eating these over the sink.

Here we are trying to be responsible and avoid the mess but the two of us ate mango after mango until that whole case was gone! We were laughing and telling stories and laughing some more. Between the two of us, we probably ate 30 mangos in that case. Let me tell you those mangos definitely didn't like me so much the next day. My mother found me under the dining room table so sick I was ready to pass out. She took me to the pediatrician and the pediatrician told my mom that I had an issue with my liver and that I would need to be on a strict diet for a month. My grandma made me food and took care of me every single day. Mangos were not on the menu. Even though it made me sick, it was worth it! That is still one of the most amazing moments of my life—spending that day eating mangos with my grandma is something I will never ever forget! Now if I want to indulge in mango, I make it into a tart and don't buy them by the case!

WHAT YOU'LL NEED

Crust

- 1 egg
- ½ cup butter, softened and cut into 1-inch cubes
- ⅔ cup granulated sugar
- ⅔ cup flour

Filling

- ½ cup Mascarpone cheese
- ½ cup heavy cream
- ½ cup powdered sugar
- ½ tsp pure vanilla extract
- 3 mangos

LET'S DO THIS!

Preheat the oven to 375°F.

For the crust: In a large bowl beat the egg, then add the butter and sugar and mix Add the flour and mix until combined—the dough will be crumbly in your hand.

Grease an eight-inch tart pan and transfer the crust mixture into it one handful at a time, pressing it down to create an even thin layer over the entire pan, about a quarter inch thick.

Freeze for about 15 minutes and reserve for later.

When you remove the crust from the freezer, prick it with a fork to prevent it from puffing when you put it in the oven. Bake the crust for 30 minutes or until golden brown.

In a mixer, mix the heavy cream until it becomes a whipped cream consistency, and it has these peaks that form, then set aside.

Use the mixer to mix the Mascarpone cheese, sugar, and pure vanilla extract until nice and smooth, then fold in the whipped heavy cream.

Once the crust is out of the oven and you have let it cool off, add this mixture to the tart.

On a cutting board, peel and cut the mangos into thin slices about a quarter inch or less, then place the mangos on top of the tart the way you prefer or as you see in the picture. Place in the refrigerator to cool down for at least 1 hour and then serve.

Too Simple Tiramisu

When I was just out of culinary school I used to work for an Italian restaurant. I became the executive chef, and the tiramisu was the most wanted dessert on the menu. We were well known for our tiramisu, but ours was an original with Marsala wine and the egg mixture being whisked. It took a long time to make it and an even longer time to let it rest. This version of tiramisu is something that I learned to make because my kids loved this dessert ever since they were little. I was always worried because it had coffee liqueur in it but let's be honest my kids have grown up on coffee so everything should be fine. I started by making it into a cupcake. Well, every time I made tiramisu cupcakes my daughter Sophia was a huge fan, so then I decided to start making this easy tiramisu to bring it to parties or have something I could make on the quick side when I am hosting as well. You can make this in less than half an hour and nobody will be able to tell that it is not a traditional style recipe.I It tastes just like it, minus all the extra work. I hope you make it. I hope you enjoy it. I hope you add extra Kahlua just like I do!

MAKES 15-18 PORTIONS **Prep time** 20 minutes | **Assembly** 10 minutes

WHAT YOU'LL NEED

- 2 cups heavy cream
- 2 cups Mascarpone cheese
- 6 tbsp granulated sugar
- 2 tsp pure vanilla extract
- 2 tbsp rum or coffee liqueur (I use Kahlua)
- 4 cups strong coffee
- 2 packages lady fingers
- cocoa powder to dust
- Optional: 4 cups brewed coffee with 2 tbsp instant espresso

LET'S DO THIS!

In a mixer, with the whisk attachment, add the heavy cream and beat until it starts forming peaks. Remove it and set aside.

In the same mixer, add the Mascarpone cheese, sugar, and pure vanilla extract and mix until nice and creamy. Add the coffee liqueur and mix until well combined. Remove from the mixer and add whipped heavy cream folding it all in until it becomes a nice and fluffy cream, set aside until time to assembly.

Open your lady fingers cookies and soak them in the coffee. Place them making a layer on the bottom of the dish.

Then spread a third of the Mascarpone mixture on top, then repeat this process for one more layer, dusting cocoa powder after each time you have spread the cream.

Once everything is set put it in the refrigerator and let it cool off for at least 1 hour. If you leave it in the refrigerator overnight it will have an even better flavor because the lady fingers will have absorbed the coffee, so this is something that you can make ahead of time.

Can't Puddin' Down Rice Pudding

When I was younger back home in Peru, my first cousin Ivan and I grew up really close, like brother and sister. I would go and spend part of my summers with him, and we have never had one fight in our entire lives. (So maybe we weren't really like brother and sister?) We got along so great and were only one year apart in age. Ivan's mom, my Aunt Carmen, was the coolest mom. She was always willing to take us anywhere and do anything with us that we wanted, no questions asked. She was just so awesome! I remember this story when one of our cousins was getting married outside of Lima where we lived. We have a big family, so we all had to go away for the weekend and stay in hotels for this big event. The day of the wedding all of the moms were getting their nails and hair done, so my Aunt Carmen took me and Ivan to have a little fun at the hotel pool. When the server came to take our drink and food order, we only wanted virgin pina colada's and we were saving our appetites for the yummy wedding food. Then the server came pushing his little dessert cart and we couldn't resist; it didn't help that the rice pudding looked so delicious (he definitely didn't need to twist our arms).

When it came and I took that first bite it was the most amazing rice pudding I had ever had in my life. I grew up on rice pudding and had many different versions, but I couldn't figure out what made this one so good and extra sweet. It couldn't be just sugar. In a blink of an eye, we had eighteen empty dishes of rice pudding (didn't I tell you that my Aunt Carmen was the coolest mom?). When the server came back, he said, "You guys really like this rice pudding huh?" I asked for the recipe, and he said the chef wouldn't be willing to share, but he did say that he used condensed milk and a good amount of pure vanilla extract. So now when I make rice pudding, I make sure it has those two ingredients. I also add raisins because a little bite of juicy sweetness never hurt anyone! But feel free to take them or leave them because it is delicious either way! The base of this rice pudding with the few secrets you are about to follow is to die for! If you wonder how the wedding story ends, my Aunt Carmen had a huge bill for rice pudding and my cousin Ivan and I had huge tummy aches. We never ate a thing at that wedding.

WHAT YOU'LL NEED

- 1 cup white rice

- 5 cups water

- 2 to 3 cinnamon sticks

- 3 cloves

- 1 can evaporated milk

- 2 cans condensed milk

- 2 tsp pure vanilla extract

- ½ cup raisins, previously soaked in water and drained

- zest 1 orange

- 1 egg yolk

- ground cinnamon

LET'S DO THIS!

In a pot, cook the rice in water with the cinnamon sticks, orange zest, and cloves. Bring it to a boil and then lower the temperature until the rice plumps up and it becomes completely cooked.

When the rice is at the right texture it won't be "al dente" but will be completely open. At this point, add the evaporated milk and stir as you continue to cook for about five minutes, then add the condensed milk, pure vanilla extract, and raisins. Cook everything together stirring constantly for another 10 minutes. It needs a little attention, but it will be so worth it!

Once the mixture is cooking, beat the egg yolk on the side, then turn off the pot of the rice mixture and add the egg yolk little by little mixing constantly so the egg doesn't cook and become scrambled eggs (what the egg yolk does is help thicken the rice pudding to the proper consistency).

Garnish with ground cinnamon on top. You can put it in the fridge to cool or serve warm

Jenny's S'mores Cups

This recipe comes from my best friend Jenny, and it's as delicious as she is beautiful. The way we met, and how our friendship started is actually a funny story. My daughter Gianna and her daughter Sydney both do competitive dance together. I grew up around dance. My Aunt Tata is a professional dance instructor and choreographer so growing up in my family if you were a girl, you danced! Jenny on the other hand is a total sports girl. She went to college playing division one soccer, so right away you know the quality of athlete she is. Coming from different backgrounds but together for the same purpose- the love of seeing our daughters do what they love the most.

On our first dance competition our age group of girls needed to wear piggy buns (the most hated hairdo by all the dance moms). I saw Jenny coming into the dressing room with Syd by her side, and Syd had crooked piggy buns. I decided to approach her, introduce myself and ask her if I could fix her buns, and Jenny said right away: "Yes please! I clearly don't know what I'm doing and I'm new here!" We both got a good laugh, a fixed hairdo, and the beginning of a friendship that I will cherish forever. Gianna and Syd are like sisters (just like Jenny and I) and something that truly brought us together is the true and honest love we have for each other. In today's world of competition and comparison, our friendship is as real and authentic as it can be. We have taught our girls since they were little the value of women supporting other women, cheering on each other's successes, and to be there when the other one needs a pick me up. Before I get any more sappy, let me tell you another thing I love about Jenny: her s'mores cups! She brought them once to one of my parties and she got me hooked! It's not only one of my favorites but also Gianna's. Jenny always makes them for her on every birthday and my only request every time is for her to make a double batch! I'm embarrassed to say I can eat about a dozen within the first few minutes she arrives. It makes my heart happy to get to pass this recipe on to you, and to share the story of the person I am proud to call my best friend.

MAKES 24 CUPS *Prep time* 20 minutes | *Cook time* 10 minutes

WHAT YOU'LL NEED

- 1 cup graham cracker crumbs

- ¼ cup powdered sugar

- 6 tbsp butter, melted

- 4 milk chocolate bars

- 12 large marshmallows

- Additional Tools: mini muffin pan

LET'S DO THIS!

Preheat the oven to 350°F.

In a small bowl, combine the graham cracker crumbs, powdered sugar, and butter.

Place 1 tablespoon of the crumb mixture in each cup of the mini muffin pan. Press the crumbs firmly to form shallow cups and bake for 4 to 5 minutes.

Remove the pan from the oven and place one Hershey's chocolate rectangle into each cup.

Cut the marshmallows in half and place one marshmallow half cut side down into each cup on top of the chocolate. Bake for 1 to 2 minutes or until marshmallows are slightly softened.

Remove the pan from the oven and cool for 15 minutes then carefully remove the cups from the pan and cool completely.

Melt the remaining Hershey's chocolate rectangles in the microwave for 1 ½ minutes until melted and smooth, stirring as necessary,

Dip the top of each marshmallow in the melted chocolate then let stand for about 1 hour or until set. You will love it!

Sophia's Cookies

Every time one of my children has a birthday, I always bake them something special. It could be a cake, cupcakes, or one of their favorite desserts. But no matter what their request is, Mommy always makes sure to give it to them. These cookies come from when my daughter Sophia was five years old, and she wanted cookies for her birthday. Oh, she didn't care about cake, she was all about the cookies. I wanted to make her delicious French butter cookies, and I remembered I had this really good recipe. I had only made them maybe once or twice, but they were melt-in-your-mouth cookies. The recipe itself is simple, but the tricky part is when you have to put the cookie dough into an actual pastry bag to be able to give them the shape that they need. Ugh.

Usually, these cookies come in a round or zig zag shape, but this time I think my dough came out a little too thick. When I was trying to make a zig zag they kept coming out as an S shape. I was so worried my daughter was going to be so disappointed. Then Sophia came walking by the kitchen and her face lit up when she saw all the cookies on my baking sheet. She was so happy, she said, "Mommy, you even made the cookies with the letter of my name!" I turned around and looked at her just going with the flow acting like I meant to do it and said, "Yes honey, I'm so glad you like them!" Even though it was a mistake, they actually turned out better than I could've imagined. It's not the shape that matters, in the end it is the effort. So, ever since that day we stopped calling them French butter cookies and started calling them Sophia's Cookies.

MAKES 30 COOKIES   *Prep time* 20 minutes | *Cook time* 15-20 minutes

WHAT YOU'LL NEED

- ¾ cup unsalted butter, room temperature

- ½ cup powdered sugar, plus 2 tbsp

- ¼ tsp salt

- ½ tsp pure vanilla extract

- 1 large egg white, room temperature

- 1 ¾ cups all-purpose flour

- To Decorate: powdered sugar or melted chocolate

LET'S DO THIS!

Preheat the oven to 350°F. Line a baking sheet with parchment paper.

In a mixer, add the butter at room temperature and mix until it is nice and creamy. Add the powdered sugar, salt, vanilla, and the egg white and mix very well. Incorporate the flour but make sure not to over mix, make sure everything is well combined but don't over mix!

Fold all the dough together and add it to a pastry bag with a star tip on the end.

On top of the lined baking sheet, spread this dough through the pastry bag in the shape of a continuous zig zag. Keep them about one and a half to two inches apart because they are going to expand when they cook.

Bake them off for about 12 to 15 minutes until they are nice and golden, but make sure you check more on the later batches as the baking sheet and oven will be hotter as you go on, so they could burn faster.

Let them cool as they come out of the oven, you can top with powdered sugar or drizzle some melted chocolate on top!

INDEX

I'm Really Grateful...

To Rich and my girls, for being the reason I want and love to cook. The smiles I have enjoyed seeing while you eat each of my meals makes my heart so full and happy.

Thank you, babe, for being an old soul and always reinforcing the time we need to spend together as a family. As much as the girls roll their eyes sometimes, they are going to remember those gatherings we spent around the table talking, laughing, and even crying. Never stop making a big deal and complimenting the easiest dishes I cook; I love to hear your voice of excitement several times over dinner letting me know how tasty it is (even though at times I think you are just using reverse psychology on me). Keep comparing my cooking to your mom's because I know it's the biggest compliment. The love and admiration you had for her melts my heart and I only wish I was lucky enough to know the woman that raised you.

Sophia, Gianna, and Alexandria, thank you for inspiring me every day. You are the reason why I want to be the best mom that I can ever be. I cherish all the meals we have cooked together, all the talks around the kitchen island, and all the dances on our kitchen floor. After all, like we like to say, "In this kitchen, we dance!" I hope one day you also cook with your children and pass down the recipes you learned with me. The idea of you having your own mom's cookbook in the kitchen is a dream come true for me.

Mom and Dad, I don't think I will ever have enough words to express the love and gratitude I have for you both. Thank you for the unconditional and obsessive love you have for me. ☺

Mom, I'm not sure what I would do without you. Not only you are my biggest cheerleader, but your daily advice and talks help me stay grounded. Those cups of coffee that you offer me when you see me working late never go unnoticed. Thank you for teaching me how to make a mean pasta sauce and for asking me to be your tester for the Pisco Sours. That's always a great job to have! LOL! Thank you for your constant help with the girls, our crazy schedules and sometimes even holding down the fort! You have allowed me to dedicate the needed time to write this book and because of you, I have the highest standards and work ethic.

Dad, the endless support and trust you show me is what fuels my soul to be the best mom to my girls as you are the best dad in the world. Believing in me and reminding me daily that I'm capable of everything and anything I can set my mind to, it's priceless. Thank you for always making me feel secure no matter which circumstances I'm in. I will never forget how you stole some of my recipes when I was in culinary school and then tried to convince me that you already made them before me. ☺ I guess that's where my competitive side comes from. I love to go on food adventures with you and explore those little holes in the wall that always surprise us with the best food! I don't need to be as "fancy" as my brother, but I enjoy food just as much!

Diego, my brother, and my parents' "golden child," I love you and your foodie heart so much! You are the best eater I know and the best oyster "sneaky" eater too! (Don't think I'm not aware of your secret trips with Dad to get oysters without me). I remember when you were one month old, and you would cry of hunger because milk just wasn't cutting it for you. Mom had to smash bananas and feed you real food! Geez! I'll never forget many Mother's Day brunches ago when you literally ate the entire raw seafood station from the restaurant. You lost your "fancy," and it was like all-you-can-eat seafood. I'm surprised the restaurant didn't go bankrupt. Cooking for you makes me challenge myself to come up with great recipes to impress you, but the truth is, no matter what, you are always excited to eat my food.

I feel so blessed that I grew up in an environment where family always came first. We all had such a tight bond, and gatherings were just a natural thing to do. We all owe that feeling and those values to my grandma: *my Mamama.* Even though she grew up in a broken home, it was never an excuse to avoid family unity. Instead, she did everything in her power to be close to her siblings, she opened the doors of her home to anyone who ever needed a place to stay, she hustled like no other to provide for my mom and siblings, and she never let anything or anyone bring her down. Her bubbly and rebel personality shined through. She wanted to see everyone succeed and will be the first one baking a cake or whipping a new dessert recipe to celebrate. Somehow, she always found a reason to celebrate (my sweet party girl!). I was lucky to enjoy her and her company more than anyone. We cooked together, took dance classes together, traveled together, anything you can imagine, I was always by her side. She spoiled me rotten, and in her eyes, I did no wrong. She embraced my rebel roots— perhaps she saw some of herself in me—and we were partners in crime! Mamama, thank you for being the angel that protects me every day. I am a firm believer that you have a VIP spot in heaven and all the blessings I receive daily, you are sending my way. I know you are so proud of me and this huge accomplishment of writing a cookbook. I'm sharing some of your recipes and our stories. I miss you so much. This one is for you!

PEOPLE WHO ROCK

Jennifer Tuma–Young

Your spirit to see women succeed it's admirable. I see the excitement in your eyes every time you speak about any of the authors in our "Inspired Girl" group. I don't think I know a bigger "girl fan" than you and I thank God for putting you in my path. I will be forever grateful for the opportunity and the reassurance you gave me in every meeting. Telling me that every-one will love this book, because in your eyes it was just SO GOOD, continuously pushed me through all the late nights of writing.

You love that I speak and write with an accent, you gave me the confidence to show people that side of me reminding me that nobody is perfect, and that's perfectly fine. Thank you for your guidance every step of the way, I always knew I could cook but I was clueless about writing. Bringing this dream of mine to life is something I'll be forever grateful to you for. I don't think even speaking two languages allow me to find the words to express what you mean to me.

Daryl Scott

Dude, I cannot think of anyone better than you to share this adventure with. You were excited and proud of me before I even asked you to help me write this book. You have helped me put my stories on paper and have translated all "my sayings" to make more sense of them. Lol! I know I drove you crazy at times, you got a lot of my sass and hard-headed ways, but you were always so supportive of my dream. If I get the opportunity to do this again, I couldn't imagine doing it with anyone but you. Thank you for not editing who I am, allowing me to be unapolo-getically myself and for your friendship. Means a lot!

Erin Kaiser

What can I say about this woman?! Your willingness to go above and beyond for any friend in need is absolutely remarkable. The love you put into everything you do is apparent and contagious. When I am overwhelmed and overworked you are always the first one in line to offer your help and encouragement. There are so many things you do for me behind the scenes, the list really is endless, but when I needed someone to help organize my photo shoots and prepare for this book launch, I couldn't have trusted anyone more than you. Your attention to detail definitely made up for my lack of organizational skills. From the bottom of my heart "Thank You" for being a friend I can always count on, and no matter what it takes or how exhausted you may be, continuing to do everything you can to help support these crazy dreams of mine. I love you!

Andrea Finn & Joanna Wallrabe

I still remember as if it was yesterday when I just finished my zoom call with Jenn and I told you I was writing a book! Your faces were priceless! Your watery eyes and hugs meant the world to me. You both mean the world to me. Your daily help and support at the barn allow me to keep growing and your words of encouragement keep me going, even when I feel like throwing in the towel. You have shared my excitement in this journey and your kind and honest friendship fills my heart.

My Oak Hill Farms Staff & Instagram Tribe

I always say that the key to happiness is to surround yourself by amazing people with awesome energy. I'm pretty lucky to have the best staff anyone can ask for, who are always willing to go that extra mile for me. No questions asked. Thank you, guys! Last but definitely not least to my Instagram tribe. You guys planted the seed . . . every time you liked and commented on my recipes, when you reshared them, when you made them, and you kept asking for more to come it's what gave me validation and the spark to get my booty in gear and go for it!

In this Kitchen, We Dance...

Playlist

1. **"Man I Feel Like a Woman"** - Shania Twain
2. **"House Party"** - Sam Hunt
3. **"1,2 Many"** - Luke Combs, Brooks & Dunn
4. **"One Margarita"** - Luke Bryan
5. **"Smoke a Little Smoke"** - Eric Church
6. **"Hackin Darts"** - Jade Eagleson
7. **"Hell On Heels"** - Pistol Annies
8. **"Heartache On the Dance Floor"** - Jon Pardi
9. **"My Church"** - Maren Morris
10. **"Mama's Broken Heart"** - Miranda Lambert
11. **"One Of Them Girls"** - Lee Brice
12. **"Country Girls (Shake It For Me)"** - Luke Bryan
13. **"Beer Never Broke My Heart"** - Luke Combs
14. **"Something Bad"** - Miranda Lambert, Carrie Underwood
15. **"Redneck Woman"** - Gretchen Wilson
16. **"Beer Can't Fix"** - Thomas Rhett, Jon Pardi
17. **"Happy Anywhere"** - Blake Shelton, Gwen Stefani
18. **"Fix a Drink"** - Chris Janson
19. **"Drink In My Hand"** - Eric Church
20. **"One Too Many"** - Keith Urban, Pink

 You Can Dance to this Playlist, too!

oak.hill.farms

Carla

Sharing my life and keepin' it real!

Living my farm dream at Oak Hill Farms.

Keep on Keepin' it Real

Website: www.oakhillfarmsnj.com

IG: @oak.hill.farms

FB: @oakhillfarmsnj

Pinterest: @oakhillfarmsnj

Tiktok: @oak.hill.farms

Published in the United States by Inspired Girl Books, a division of Inspired Girl Enterprises, New Jersey.
www.inspiredgirlenterprises.com
www.inspiredgirlbooks.com

Recipes Developed by: Carla Bushey
Editorial & Creative Director: Jenn Tuma-Young
Lead Graphic Designer: Jasmine Hromjak
Content Editor: Daryl Scott
Copy Editor: Janelle Leonard
Photo Shoot Location 1: Content + Company
Photo Shoot Location 2: The Bushey Home
Photo Shoot Location 3: Oak Hill Farms
Photographer: Louise O'Rourke
Location Hosts Location 1: Courtney & John Achilli
On-Set Stylist Location 1: Erin Kaiser
On-Set Stylist Locations 2 and 3: Destini Locorriere
Makeup Artist Locations 2 and 3: Jenn Cappella

Library of Congress Number: 2021915266
ISBN: 978-1-7373163-3-6

Printed and Bound in the United States of America.